Old Bank –
New Bank

*The First National Bank,
Houston*

1866-1956

Old Bank–
New Bank

The First National Bank, Houston

1866-1956

William A. Kirkland

PACESETTER PRESS
A Division of Gulf Publishing Company
Houston, Texas

Old Bank—New Bank
The First National Bank,
Houston, 1866-1956

Library of Congress Catalog Card Number 74-27681
ISBN 0-88415-304-5

Contents

Foreword

Oldest Bank Now Newest in Houston!

That was the amazing headline in the Houston press of May 3, 1933. As of the close of business on May 2nd, the First National Bank *of* Houston, born within a year after the Civil War, had agreed to transfer its sound assets and deposit liabilities to First National Bank *in* Houston. So, at 9:00 a.m. the next morning, May 3, the successor bank opened for business, a newly chartered institution with Capital Stock of $3,000,000, Surplus of $600,000, and Undivided Profits of $150,000. On the surface nothing was different, familiar officers were at their desks to serve the customers, the Board of Directors of the new institution exactly the same as of the old. But, it was true. A new First National had taken over. In its design, in its working, and in the result accomplished the reorganization proved to be unique. No other bank reorganization has been comparable to it in concept, execution, or final triumph.

It was difficult for the public then or now to believe that something had happened to the First National Bank, a veteran of many ups and downs since the 1860's and long the largest bank in Houston. Shock there was but never a run. Generations of fair and considerate and constructive dealings had built up public confidence that may have wavered but did not crack. And later, rebounding from the depression years and growing with Houston's war time and post war economy, the Bank was in a strong position to join with the City National in 1956 to form the First City National Bank.

Since 1956 the distinctive character and personality that was the First National Bank has been absorbed and diffused throughout the corporate structure of the First City. From 1866 to 1956, however, it was a landmark financial institution in the State of Texas. The first bank in Houston to possess a national charter, it was run for many years by one man, B.A. Shepherd, and after Mr. Shepherd's death in 1891 it continued to reflect the Shepherd family interest. Having grown up in Houston and having spent my career with First National Bank since 1920 and having served as its president at the time of the merger in 1956, I knew first hand virtually all of those who in this century directed its affairs. Records that go back to the time of incorporation have helped piece together salient features of the bank's earlier history.

Also of great help to me have been the research and the reports of the late Edwin A. Bonewitz, a local historian of painstaking industry and accuracy, and of my long associate as vice-president of the First National, the late Carl C. Hall who handled the Bank's publicity for many years. Among other former teammates and bank officials who have preserved and made available to me the oldest records of the institution together with their encouragement are Albert E. Cleere and Britt Bruner, while devoted secretarial services beyond the call of regular duty have been provided me by Mrs. Ruth Wolf and Miss Nettie Buddendorff, both First National veterans, and by Mrs. Thelmarie Ward of First City National. Many times have I taken advantage of the assistance of Mrs. Mary Flo Ulmer and of Mrs. Marian Branon, her successor as head of the Texas Room in the Houston Public Library. The courtesies of Mrs. Marilyn Sibley, Professor of History, Houston Baptist University, and of James A. Tinsley, Professor of History, University of

Houston, in reading the manuscript and making valuable suggestions were very helpful indeed. To all I extend my acknowledgement of indebtedness and my hearty thanks.

William A. Kirkland
Houston, Texas
March, 1975

A National Bank
in Houston
in 1865?

The history of the First National Bank of Houston properly begins with the wartime banking legislation of 1863 and
1864 and the postwar efforts to mend economic institutions
torn asunder by the Civil War. The National Banking Act
permitted the federal government to grant corporate
charters to banks and thereby institutionalize and expand
badly needed banking services. By the time General Lee surrendered to General Grant at Appomattox on April 9, 1865,
over 1000 national banks had been authorized, including one
in the conquered city of New Orleans. By October 1 of that
same year, twenty national banks had been chartered in
Southern states that had been in conflict with the Union.
Thirteen of these were in Virginia, where a reconstruction
government acceptable to the Federal Congress had been
quickly set up.

Then, four days before his death on April 15th, President
Lincoln displayed in his remarks to a crowd celebrating the
collapse of the Confederacy an attitude of understanding and
reconciliation towards the South. His successor, President
Andrew Johnson, proclaimed considerate reconstruction
policies. All were later swept away by a vengeful Congress,

but it appears that from the first the Secretary of the Treasury and his Comptroller of the Currency wasted little time in splitting legal hairs as to the status of the defeated states, most of whom were unrepresented in Congress and soon to be occupied by federal troops. They quickly acted in the interest of the nation and granted bank charters to responsible groups in key Southern cities whose members had received presidential pardons or had taken the Amnesty Oath.

The Secretary of the Treasury at this time was Hugh McCulloch (1808-95), a banker-lawyer who in 1863 resigned from the presidency of the State Bank of Indiana in Fort Wayne to accept appointment by President Lincoln as the first Comptroller of the Currency under the new National Banking Act. He had become the Secretary at the beginning of President Lincoln's second term and remained in office under President Johnson. In his annual report for the fiscal year ended June 30, 1866, McCulloch explained his policy (a sort of a Marshall Plan for the South):

Now as the Government has assumed entire control of the currency of the country involving a direct supervision of its banking interests, it becomes the duty of the Government to provide adequate banking facilities to all sections.

The States lately in rebellion, not being in a condition to avail themselves of the privileges granted in the National Banking Act at the time when they were offered, and when it was still possible to obtain them, are now left almost entirely destitute of currency and banking facilities. This deficiency is the occasion of great inconvenience and loss to the people of those States and it is very desirable for many reasons that it should be supplied.

First, it is important to all sections, particularly to the North, that the South be supplied with all facilities necessary for production of its great staple crops because their export reduces export of gold.

Second, capital in large part is being supplied by foreign capitalists who gain control over a large proportion of valuable products, taking larger profits to themselves and leaving the country barely the cost of production. This, naturally, causes much discontent and dissatisfaction among the producers.

Third, prosperous industry is the most speedy and certain remedy for the existing evils in the Southern States. It will allay bitterness of feeling, dissatisfaction with the results of the war, and promote contentment among the people. The assistance that could be rendered for the promotion of this end by local banking associations would be important both in character and extent. Besides, a community of financial and pecuniary interests would bring into exercise an element of great power for the assimilation of the aims, purposes and hopes of all the people of all the states. The extension of the national banking system throughout the entire Union would bring about such an identity of interests in the credit of the Government and of the entire system of banks as would secure the active and zealous cooperation of all sections toward the preservation of such credit unimpaired.

In his 1867 report a year later, Secretary McCulloch stated the case in straighter, simpler terms:

The importance of the restoration of the Southern States cannot be overestimated. The great staples of the South have for many years constituted a large portion of our total exports. But for cotton held there at the close of the war, foreign exchanges against the United States would have made commercial convulsion unavoidable. Despite deplorable conditions last year more than two-thirds of United States exports were from Southern states. This year's poor crop will save the United States from ruinous indebtedness to Europe.

The Secretary's messages showed vision and courage and a certain broad sympathy for the plight of the southern people. But it is clear that over a century ago the Treasury's overriding concern was the same one confronting the Secretary of the Treasury today—to provide an effective solution to the balance of payments problem. The other issue to which the Secretary indirectly addressed himself—the constitutional question of whether or not the Southern states were entitled to the benefits of federal wartime banking legislation—was settled affirmatively by the Supreme Court in the case of Texas *vs.* White in 1869. In Texas *vs.* White, Chief Justice Chase rendered in April, 1869, the following opinion of the Court: "That in the Articles of Confederation the Union had been declared to be perpetual; that the Constitution contained the phrase: 'to form a more perfect union'; that the Ordinances of Secession, though adopted by a convention in Texas and ratified by a majority of the citizens, were null; that the State did not cease to be a state; that indeed Texas continued to be a state and a state of the Union."

The first attempt to found a national bank in Houston originated with a Galvestonian. In mid-1865 applications had already been filed in Washington for two national banks for the City of Galveston. Knowing this, Benjamin F. McDonough of Galveston imagined that the growing trading community of Houston would support one of these federally chartered institutions. During the Civil War McDonough had been stationed at Sabine Pass, Texas, as an assessor of internal revenue for the Confederate government.

In August of 1865 McDonough, who seems to have been a kinsman of President Andrew Johnson, went to Washington City to obtain a pardon for his activities as a "rebel" and to seek appointment to a federal office. On August 17 he applied to the Comptroller of the Currency "in behalf of myself and associates, residents of Houston, Texas" for permission to organize "a national bank in the City of Houston with a capital of $100,000." According to his own statements later, he had never been engaged in banking, he had not spoken to anyone in Houston about his project and he had no associates there, but "expected to get them on my return to Texas." Apparently his application was accepted and material for a formal presentation was supplied him.

Two days later on August 19, 1865, Lorenzo Sherwood, a lawyer with an office at 24 Pine Street, New York, signed for himself and under a power of attorney for B.F. McDonough a request of the Comptroller, soon granted, to amend the application to reflect a proposed capital for the new bank of $300,000 instead of $100,000. As interested with him and McDonough in this petition, Sherwood listed several "loyal citizens of Houston," among them Dr. Ingham S. Roberts, a Union sympathizer and Chief Justice of Harris County, Texas, of which Houston is the county seat. At that time McDonough himself had never met Dr. Roberts or any of the others who were named. Exactly how Sherwood of New York and McDonough of Galveston came together in Washington

Washington D.C.
Augt 17th 1865

Sir:

On behalf of myself and associates,
citizens of Houston, Texas, I desire here
within to organize a National Bank
in the City of Houston, with a capital
of $100,000. and will respectfully ask to
be furnished with the necessary forms and
blanks for that purpose.

Very Respectfully
B. F. M. Lonough

Hon Freeman Clarke
Comptroller of the Currency

Only four months after General Robert E. Lee's surrender McDonough, a Galvestonian, filed the first application for a nationally chartered bank for Houston with $100,000 capital.

*In the matter of the application for a
National Bank at Houston, Texas:
To the Hon the Comptroller of the Currency —
The undersigned B. F. McDonough and Lorenzo Sher-
wood, in Connection with Wm J. Hutchings, Chauncy B. Sabin
Dr Roberts, Mr Morris, and others loyal Citizens of
the State of Texas desire to Establish a National
Bank at the City of Houston in the State of Texas
with a Capital of Three Hundred Thousand Dollars,
And request permission to Establish the Same
accordingly —
Dated August 19, 1865 —*

*B. F. McDonough By
L. Sherwood*

Lorenzo Sherwood —

*Two days later a New York lawyer representing Houston people
hoping to organize a national bank, persuaded McDonough to join
in a $300,000 project and obtained his power of attorney to amend
the application. (See exhibits above and on next page)*

and decided to collaborate is uncertain. Undoubtedly they
were known to each other because Sherwood, an able, elo-
quent but controversial political economist, had practiced
law in Galveston for fifteen years prior to the Civil War and
had served a stormy term in the Texas legislature. One could
surmise that Sherwood, well known as a Unionist with a
political background in New York and Texas, had helped

In the matter of the Establishment of
a National Bank at Houston Texas.
The Comptroller of the Currency will
please allow Mr Sherwood to use my
name in Connection with the increase
of the Capital ~~proposed~~ for the national
Bank proposed to be Established at
Houston, Texas —
Aug. 20. 1865 —
B F McDonough

with the two Galveston applications then being processed, and perhaps some in other states. This is borne out by his having available a preprinted form with which to establish correspondent relationships between his client would-be banks and the Fourth National Bank of New York located at 29 Pine Street, just across the street from his office.

A probability is that Sherwood, described by Dr. Roberts as his Eastern correspondent, had been employed to represent a group of Houston citizens bent on obtaining the first national charter for their town. However, when he arrived in Washington with his Houston clients' application, he was surprised to find that an acquaintance from Galveston had beaten him to it. He must have recognized at once an opportunity to merge the interests of Dr. Robert's group with that of President Johnson's cousin and thus share in the priority and the political influence behind it. Undoubtedly, he persuaded McDonough that the raising of even more capital for his bank would be greatly facilitated by an alliance with influential Houston people whose names, Dr. Roberts later stated, were supplied by him "at the instance of Mr. Sherwood and other Union friends in Washington and New York." But, to be on the safe side indeed, Sherwood managed to obtain from the Comptroller a set of charter application forms identical with those that had been given to McDonough, and this second set seems to have been promptly forwarded to Dr. Roberts.

From the Houston end Dr. Roberts swiftly followed up with a communication dated September 12, 1865, referring to the application of McDonough and Sherwood and certifying to the Comptroller that organization of First National Bank of Houston "with true and loyal men" had been set in motion and would be consummated with all reasonable dispatch. This certificate was signed by the doctor and six other Houstonians but not, significantly, by McDonough. When this paper reached the Comptroller's office in Washington, the Comptroller pencilled across its face, "Where is McDonough?" As a matter of fact, that gentleman's later actions suggest that from the beginning he had not intended to

Houston, Texas,
Sept 12th 1865,

To. Hon Hugh McCulloch
Comptroller of Currency,
Washington D.C,

Sir,
Application has been made to your Department, by Messrs B. F. McDonough, and Lorenzo Sherwood Esqrs in the names of I. S. Roberts, Chauncey B. Sabin, I. R. Morris, D. S. Baldwin and William I. Hutchins, for the privilege of establishing a National Bank in the City of Houston, with a capital of $300.000 ...

a Bank, under the name of "The First National Bank of Houston," in the city of Houston, County of Harris, State of Texas.

Very Respectfully
Your Obt. Servts.

J. S. Roberts
Wm. Clark
D. G. Baldwin
C. B. Sabin
W. R. Baker
J. R. Morris
James Purse
Wm. B. McDonough

New York Sept. 30. 1865.

Hon. F. Clark
Comptr. of the Currency — Washington D.C.

I am happy to state that in my belief the application for the Bank at Houston will be carried to a Consummation with all reasonable despatch.

Very truly &c
Lorenzo Sherwood —

This shows a portion of instrument of September 12, 1865 following up the charter application which was sent to Lawyer Sherwood in New York. Adding his endorsement, he presented it to the Comptroller of the Currency, who wrote in pencil, shown here faintly, "Where is McDonough?" Only three of the persons named above had actually subscribed to stock in the bank when it opened.

subscribe to stock in a bank or in any way to participate in its formal establishment. There is good reason to believe that McDonough had used his influence with the President of the United States solely in expectation of substantial compensation as finder and promoter.

Returning from Washington City to Texas, B.F. McDonough brought with him his pardon at the hand of the President, his appointment as Collector of Internal Revenue, First District of Texas, at Galveston, and his set of application papers, "a copy of the banking laws and printed forms," which he took to constitute prior and exclusive permission to organize a national bank in Houston. It is not certain that he was fully aware of what Lorenzo Sherwood had done in his name, for he arrived in Houston in order, as he put it, "to find some party wishing to engage in banking." However, in due course he did go to one of Sherwood's clients, William Clark, a merchant, who soon would introduce him to Dr. Roberts. Thereafter, these three—McDonough, Clark and Roberts together with some nonresident friends of McDonough, began to solicit stock subscriptions. The raising of $300,000 of capital proved to be impossible. The goal was reduced to $150,000, and when it could not be reached at that level the printed forms were altered a second time to represent a bank of $100,000 capital. As early as September 20, 1865, the preliminary form thus adjusted for this much smaller enterprise was executed by a number of representative local businessmen, almost all of whom became stockholders in a successful attempt which did not begin until six months later. This form, like previous papers, lacked the signature of McDonough; nor did any of his nonresident associates sign. It was not mailed straightway to Washington but went first to New York to Sherwood, who added his endorsement and filed it with the Comptroller. The effort failed.

Why this promising attempt to form the bank came to naught is not clear. Perhaps there was truth in the hints, possibly passed to Washington, that local interests resented McDonough and his out-of-town associates, with whom they had been suddenly merged, and intended somehow to bypass them. At any rate, early in 1866 Roberts and Clark started

First National Bank of Houston.

---·+·---

ARTICLES OF AGREEMENT.

WE THE UNDERSIGNED, do hereby severally agree to. take the number of Shares, of One Hundred Dollars each, set opposite to our respective names, of the stock of an Association to be organized by the subscribers hereto, or by those to whom the stock shall be awarded, under the act of Congress of the United States of America, entitled " An Act to provide a National Currency secured by a pledge of United States Bonds, and to provide for the circulation and redemption thereof," approved July 3d, 1864, and the amendment thereto. Such Association shall be called the

FIRST NATIONAL BANK OF HOUSTON.

The capital stock of said Bank is fixed at ~~One~~ HUNDRED THOUSAND DOLLARS, with the privilege of increasing the same to the extent of Hundred Thousand Dollars, whenever a majority of the stockholders may deem it fit for the interest of the Association so to do : And we do hereby constitute and appoint *B. A. McDonough and J. B. Likens of Galveston, John A. Lamfred, Washington County, and W. Clarke and J. Sherwood* of the City of Houston, ...ssioners to receive subscriptions for the capital stock of such Association ; and in case more a. ~~Two~~ One Hundred Thousand Dollars shall be subscribed, to award the same to such subscribers, or to apportion the same among the subscribers as they shall deem best.

Printed pursuant to the application of McDonough and Sherwood, this form dated September 30, 1865 for signing by all prospective stockholders, called for $300,000 capital. Sale of stock was slow. The proposed capital was reduced by ink amendment to $150,000 and then to $100,000.

again with McDonough's application forms, building up new hopes of success with about the same group of stock subscribers, provided W.J. Hutchins, the richest man in the town, would agree to be bank president. However, McDonough suddenly became suspicious of competition and, charging undue delay, demanded the return of his papers. Thereupon, Dr. Roberts, fairly certain of an affirmative answer from Hutchins within twenty-four hours, bought that additional time by signing for McDonough, on that date, January 20, 1866, a promise to give him in the event the particular effort should succeed, $3,000 in stock at the time of official organization and $5,000 in currency at the opening of the bank. When on the next day Hutchins refused to become involved, Roberts and Clark admitted defeat and returned the printed forms to McDonough. However, they neglected to recover the written agreement. That paper became the basis of twelve years of litigation, the records of which contain most of these facts and quotations. McDonough and his friends made one last endeavor to get the capital stock subscribed, this time in Washington County, Texas, a prosperous cotton-growing section some seventy-five miles to the northwest. When that fell through they returned to their respective homes, and McDonough disconsolately dropped the application papers off at William Clark's mercantile office as he passed through Houston on his way to Galveston.

Weeks later one William Fulton, a merchant who had not previously shown interest, took the matter in hand and personally passed around for signatures a new stock subscription form. Then at his instance an outstanding man of affairs, J.T. Brady, called an organization meeting for February 15, 1866. The stock had by then been fully subscribed for a $100,000 bank. At that meeting of prospective stockholders nine directors were elected, including Dr. Roberts because he was known to be a Unionist and thus was qualified to execute an affidavit to the integrity and loyalty of the others, all undoubtedly Confederate sympathizers. On the following day the directors met and elected officers, subject of course to the official acceptance in Washington.

The officers were T.M. Bagby, president; R.S. Willis, vice-president; and William N. Cooke, cashier. The first Board of Directors included Bagby and Willis and seven others: J.T. Brady, William Clark, William Fulton, S.L. Hohenthal, H.R. Percy, M. Reichman and Dr. Ingham S. Roberts. Subscribers to the $100,000 capital of the bank were forty-four persons of diverse business and professional activities.

Bagby, a Virginian, had arrived in Houston in 1837 at the age of 23. He was employed in local stores until he es-

I Ingham S. Roberts Chief Justice of Harris Co. hereby Certify that the Stock holders of the First National Bank Houston have taken the Amnesty Oath as prescribed by the Secretary of State of the United States and where Presidential Pardons were necessary and applied for, have received said Pardons and have in Every respect followed the requirements of The Banking Law to the best of their knowledge and belief.

Given at the City of Houston the 1st day of March 1866

Ingham S. Roberts Chf. Just. Harris Co. Texas

By the date shown here a proper application executed by persons subscribing to $100,000 in stock was pending in the Office of the Comptroller. The Chief Justice of Harris County, a Unionist, certified to the eligibility of the applicants.

tablished his own office as "Cotton Factor and Planters' Commission Merchant." Mr. Willis was his brother's partner in the mercantile firm of P.J. Willis & Bro., then of Houston, later of Galveston. The other directors were merchants, agents for receiving and forwarding goods on commission, two auctioneers, a lawyer and a county official. John T. Brady was perhaps the outstanding businessman of the group. A native of Maryland with legal training, Brady reached Houston in 1856, served in the State Legislature and Senate, originated the Texas State Fair, and had the first dreams of a belt railway and deep-water facilities for the city.

Among the more prominent original stockholders were Henry R. Allen, a brother of Houston's founders, John K. and A.C. Allen; Paul Bremond, the successful railroad builder; and T.W. House, a baker boy from England who began a few years after arrival here to build a bakery and confectionery shop into a wholesale house. His incidental banking activities became a separate department after the Civil War and later developed into an outstanding private bank. Among other stockholders were lawyer Peter W. Gray, son of William Fairfax Gray, official in the First Legislature of the Republic of Texas and founder of Houston's Christ Church, Episcopal; E.W. Cave, Secretary of State in 1860-61 in Sam Houston's only term as governor; and E.H. Cushing, editor of the *Houston Telegraph*. Also on the roster were some whose names are still familiar to Houstonians—men such as Berleth, Dumble, Grainger, Macatee, Milby, Pettit, Reynaud, and Schneider.

The organization of the group seeking the bank charter and succeeding at it had finally been effected independently of any connection with McDonough, but it is true that he and several of his nonsubscriber friends were present at the meeting. There was no record of their having played any part in the proceedings, and it has been determined that nothing was said in the presence of stockholders or directors or to any of the individuals separately about McDonough's little paper called a "contract" which had been signed by Dr. Roberts presumably in connection only with the earlier and unsuccessful effort.

After taking the preliminary steps of organizing the prospective stockholders to elect directors and the directors to choose officers by mid-February, 1866, promoters of the First National Bank of Houston were so confident of Federal approval that they went immediately to work to be ready for banking operations. They rented quarters in a narrow two-story brick building on the west side of Main Street between

Treasury Department,
Office of Comptroller of the Currency
Washington March 19, 1866.

In the matter of the First National Bank of Houston in the State of Texas —

I hereby certify that I am personally acquainted with most of the Stockholders subscribing the Capital Stock in the above Bank, and am acquainted by reputation with all of them; that they are business men of great pecuniary responsibility, and of high integrity; and as to loyalty to the government I am fully satisfied that they are doing what they can to sustain the government and to inculcate a healthy spirit in the State where they reside. I have no hesitation in recommending the grant of their application for a Bank —

With Very High respect, I am
Very Respectfully Yours

Hon Freeman Clarke
Comptr of the Currency

Lorenzo Sherwood

The New York lawyer adds his testimony to the substance and loyalty of the stock subscribers.

Preston and Prairie Avenues, owned incidentally by the wife of Dr. Roberts. They prepared bylaws, procured and approved a corporation seal and voted to send a stockholder, Muter Miller, as official representative to Washington City. Designated as special agent, Miller was empowered to make

Resolved that Mr. Muter Miller be and is hereby appointed the Special Agent for the First National Bank of Houston to proceed to Washington City for the purpose of making the necessary deposit of Funds with the Comptroller of the Currency file the evidence of organization and procure the proper certificate of Authority for the Bank to begin its business — Also that he be authorised to proceed to New York and procure the necessary Safes, Desks, Iron Crib, for Vault, Books, and other Furniture proper for the business of Banking — and that the President and Secretary furnish him with a Copy of this Resolution signed by them as evidence of his authority, and such letters as may be necessary for him to act for the Bank in all matters of formality required to complete the organisation according to law and the instructions of the Secretary of the Treasury

Resolved that Mr. Muter Miller be authorised to make Financial Arrangements with the Banks at New Orleans & New York for the First National Bank of Houston

T. M. Bagby
President

Wm. Fulton
Cashier.

A Special Agent was appointed March 1, 1866 to complete the requirements of the Secretary of Treasury and to obtain the necessary authority for the bank to open for business.

the necessary deposit of funds with the Comptroller of the Currency, to obtain "the final Certificate of Authority" for the Bank to begin its business and, if successful thus far, to purchase in New York "safes, desks, iron cribs for vaults, books and furniture" and to make financial arrangements with banks in both New York and New Orleans. At that point Dr. Roberts, still impressed with McDonough's supposed influence with President Johnson, recommended that he be asked to accompany Miller. It was so ordered by the Board and McDonough agreed to go, without special compensation but with his expenses paid. He later explained that he had been willing to assist on that basis "on account of the document I had signed, by Dr. Roberts—I don't know that any of the directors knew of the Roberts paper except Roberts himself. He was the only one I ever talked to about it."

Miller was given all necessary papers, including an affidavit by Dr. Roberts that the stockholders of the would-be bank had "taken the Amnesty Oath as prescribed by the Secretary of State of the United States and where Presidential pardons were necessary and had been applied for have received said pardons." In early March Miller went to Galveston with a letter of introduction to McDonough, whom strangely he had not met, and together they proceeded to Washington. Lorenzo Sherwood joined them there to act as political guide and to put in the Comptroller's file his written assurance of the character and responsibility of the Houston people. The Comptroller of the Currency did ask again why McDonough, the original applicant, was not listed among the stockholders of the bank seeking charter approval. McDonough said nothing but Special Agent Miller, with help from Sherwood, convinced the official that "it was all right."

However, before granting the charter, the Comptroller of the Currency required that the prospective bank waive all claim to the privilege of issuing its own circulating currency. On March 21 Miller signed a stipulation to that effect and promised to back it up with a resolution of the Board of Directors on his return to Houston. On the strength of this promise it was directed that the bank be permitted to open for business, and the Certificate of Organization was issued the next day. Moving on to New York, Miller arranged a correspondent bank relationship with the National Park Bank and purchased the various articles of equipment authorized. Then, giving McDonough $1,000 (twice what he asked for) to cover his expenses, he shortly headed back to Houston alone. He stopped off at New Orleans to complete his mission and he died suddenly while there. In the Directors' minutes of April 3, 1866, the only pertinent entry reads: "The sad news of the death of Mr. Miller was given to the Board."

Today the delivery of a charter for a national bank is made by a representative of the Comptroller simultaneously with the opening of the bank for business. Not so in 1866. It was May 15 before the Cashier, William N. Cooke, who had been selected from a field of several candidates as the only paid officer, was able to certify to the Comptroller that as much as $91,550 had been "paid in on account of the capital stock," and it was May 21 before the balance of the $100,000 capital was in hand and reported to Washington. Nevertheless, the authority to do business had been granted back on March 22 and on May 16 the bank did open. By the end of the first business day the cashier had accepted four deposits, all in coin, totaling $12,618.70. Within a week a number of new customers had been added, bringing total deposits to $110,138.40, including only $161 in currency. One deposit, that of P.J. Willis & Bro. on May 18, amounted to $80,361.25, every bit of it in coin. In June a $7,000 account was opened under the style of John B. Root, Cashier, which, surprisingly enough for so early a day, set up a correspondent bank relationship with the first national bank in Texas, the First National Bank of Galveston, for which Root was acting.

It was not until the morning of July 4, according to the minute book, that the directors met to take note of the progress being made. Then, after appointing a committee of three to examine the safes and to see if the amount of cash on hand agreed with the statement rendered by the Cashier, they adjourned until 8:00 o'clock in the evening. When they reassembled they learned from the committee that the amount of money reported by the cashier tallied with the amount of money in the safe and then resolved that the president and cashier be bonded to the extent of $20,000. At

Treasury Department,
Office of Comptroller of the Currency
Washington 21st March 1866

The First National Bank of Houston stipulates to waive all claim to Circulation under the Act of Congress approved June 3d 1864 limiting the National Currency to Three hundred Millions of Dollars :—

Mister Miller
Stock holder, and authorized Agent of the First National Bank

Mr. Miller agrees to send a resolution of the Board of Directors waiving all claim to circulation and Mr. Clarke directs the Bank to be organized
O Connell

On the strength of this agreement by the Special Agent, a charter was granted on March 22, 1866. Mr. Miller died before he returned to Houston, and there is no record that the promised resolution was ever passed.

the same time they established banking hours so as to commence business at 9:00 a.m. and to close at 3:00 p.m., a practice that was not changed for Houston banks until a Clearing House action on March 20, 1933.

Very soon it was recognized that the earning power of the institution was handicapped by its lack of the privilege of increasing loanable funds through issuance of its own bank notes. Before the bank was five months old Vice-President

Willis, on a business trip to New York, stopped by Washington and successfully negotiated for the authority to issue currency. There is no record that the directors ever passed the resolution promised by Special Agent Miller when he signed in the Comptroller's office a stipulation waiving for the Bank the right of circulation of its own currency. Willis had wiped out that obligation and when the Board received his report they extended him thanks plus $50 towards the expenses of his Washington visit.

The first annual meeting of stockholders was held on January 7, 1867, and the number of directors was reduced from nine to seven. Four of those elected to the Board were from the original group—Messrs. Bagby, Hohenthal, Percy and Willis. Three were new ones—R. Brewster, G.A. Forsgard and B.A. Shepherd. It is hard to understand why the stockholders preferred a smaller directorate and why Brady and Fulton, prime organizers, were among those who failed of re-election. The earlier connection of Dr. Roberts and Clark with McDonough, the promoter, may have carried weight in the cases of their elimination. No matter; the important action at this meeting was the recognition of Shepherd as too able a businessman and banker not to be added. Indeed, he immediately proved to be the key man in the picture, dominating and running the Bank for twenty-five years.

At the directors' meeting which followed, the officers, Messrs. Bagby, Willis and Cooke, were re-elected but with no increase in pay "because the financial condition of the bank did not justify." (The cashier was being paid $4,000 in currency per annum and the bookkeeper and teller $2,500 each.) Although the by-laws called for the board to meet monthly, the directors designated Thursday as the "Day of Discount" and decided that they should meet every Wednesday at 6:00 p.m. to "examine offerings." Today we would call them "loan applications." At a series of Wednesday evening meetings early in 1867 the question of new quarters for the Bank proved the first item for discussion. The rented banking space in the fifth block of Main Street had become less than adequate, and a committee was authorized to offer A. Sessums $15,000 for the building at the southeast corner of

Main and Franklin. The negotiations with Sessums continued for a while but, though he was willing to sell, he insisted upon conditions that were unacceptable. So nothing came of that idea, at least not for fifteen years, and on May 1 the directors were informed that space in a building on Congress and Fannin had been rented from Eugene Pillot for $80 in gold per month but only until January 1, 1868.

Meanwhile the Bank had been visited by a national bank examiner, the first evidence of the federal supervision so routine but valuable today. It was one J.T. Copley to whom, at the end of his inspection, a vote of thanks was recorded in view of his "helpful suggestions and his gentlemanly and urbane manner." In April the directors, recognizing that the president was called upon to give considerable time to the business of the bank, voted Bagby a salary of $1,500 per annum retroactive to January. At no time did the minutes make any mention of directors' fees. In fact, none were paid during the entire life of this institution. On the contrary, at this meeting a fine of $2.50 was instituted, to be imposed on any director missing two consecutive meetings unless for good and sufficient reasons.

In mid-June Bagby tendered his resignation as president. On July 1, 1867, his resignation was accepted, though he continued as a director, and B.A. Shepherd was elected to succeed him. Shepherd, with years of experience in business and banking in Houston, agreed to merge B.A. Shepherd and Company's Banking Exchange and Collection Office with the new federally chartered institution. At the same meeting Cooke resigned as cashier, and A. Wettermark, Shepherd's banking partner, was elected to take his place.

Private Bank
Takes Over

Benjamin Armistead Shepherd, born in 1814 on a Virginia farm some miles from Charlottesville, left home in 1833, worked his way across the mountains, down the Ohio River, and up the Cumberland to Nashville, Tennessee, where he found employment in a wholesale establishment. After a few years there and a year or two in New Orleans, he landed in Galveston in 1839 at the age of 25. Almost at once, with a few dollars saved from his wages, he helped organize the mercantile firm of Crawford and Shepherd, and in 1844 moved his family to Houston to manage the branch house opened there two years before under the name of Shepherd and Crawford. Soon A.J. Burke, later mayor of the city, bought out Crawford's Houston interest, and the firm became the independent enterprise of Shepherd and Burke. Like all merchants, they had to do a considerable credit business. Interior merchants and planters paid up their accounts in the fall by sending in cotton and other produce to be sold on commission. More often than not, this procedure involved interest charges and in season the simple banking function of holding money for the account of customers. In 1854 the sale of the business to Burke left Shepherd free to open a separate office to conduct a banking operation all his own.

Shepherd was a director of the Commercial and Agricultural Bank during its twelve years of successful business from 1847 to 1859. This was the first chartered bank in Texas which, after more than a decade of work and planning on the part of its promoters, finally opened its doors in Galveston in December, 1847. Its charter, originally granted in 1835 by the Mexican State of Coahuila and Texas under the style of Banco de Comercio Y Agricultura with the privileges of establishing branches and of issuing its own currency, was recognized by the Republic of Texas and later duly confirmed by the legislature of the state of Texas. Constantly under political attack by enemies of chartered banking in any form, it was finally in 1859 forced by a decision of the Supreme Court of Texas to go out of business. From its Galveston headquarters it had issued currency and had met all of its obligations with honor and profit, maintaining a branch in Brownsville, Texas, and agencies in New York, New Orleans, and Akron, Ohio. Its affairs were transferred to Ball, Hutchings and Co. of Galveston, organized in 1854.

Because of this banking experience and his familiarity with local credits gained as a merchant, Shepherd met with growing success in his private banking operations. But when Texas, against his personal conviction, chose secession from the Union he decided not to have responsibility for the funds of others. He therefore paid off his depositors in coin and closed his bank. Some of his liquid assets remained frozen in New York or were transferred to a sterling account with Baring Brothers of London. During the war years that followed he served the Confederate government in various ways involving cotton and other merchandise. But, within a year after peace came, he re-entered the banking business with a notice carried daily in the newspapers in the spring of 1866: "B.A. Shepherd will reopen on May 1st for the resumption of his old business of Banker and Exchange Dealer which he commenced here 15 years ago and promises to give all the attention to his friends and correspondents that his physical ability will permit."

In 1866 Shepherd was well aware of the impending opening of the First National Bank of Houston. In letters to Wettermark, a young associate of the prewar days, and to a nephew in Nashville, both of whom he hoped to attract to be junior partners, he made frequent reference to the new competition and hastened to get ahead of it. In March he wrote: "True, the country is filling with national banks, but I fancy they need not be feared very seriously. Capital and brains will tell outside of them as well as in"; in April, "I am going to work as soon as I can get an office to do it in"; and, "First National Bank opens here about 1 May. My friends tell me and it's my judgment to start first. No doubt of my sure success despite any such seeming opposition, for there is no one engaged in the concern who knows much about it."

By May he was back in business as private banker, reporting: "Since 1 May I have been going on with my old business," and, "I feel that I am a fixture here for the balance of my life and will work with that view. I feel that I can do nearly as great a job in business here as I ever did—notwithstanding the national banks, judging from appearances so far. I have received in deposits in gold in the four days I have been opened about $100,000 and I think it not unlikely that by the first of June it will be $200,000." Of course, First National did open on May 16, and in August Shepherd commented on his banking neighbor: "In the first place I was bored to death nearly by the parties here getting up the First National Bank to take the Presidency of it at a salary of $10,000 per year in gold. This was a tempting offer as I know that with their capital they could afford to do it and it would last, but then it would involve the breaking up and involving all my old business in that it was doubtless part of the consideration. But I declined it believing I could beat them all along by myself and I have, I suppose, more in deposits, exchange and everything, maybe double theirs. I know I have had a good thing started here and I feel that I ought to continue it for some of my own kin who could attend to the business and keep it going without any falling off in the ability of conducting it;" and, "Speaking of which I may remark that the Bank (First National) has not been in my way at all and I think the Insurance Company will be quite as small an obstacle in my way. Somehow I find people are inclined to extend me a preference."

The Houston Insurance Company to which Shepherd referred was active in banking as well as insurance. It was located in 1868 at the northeast corner of Main and Franklin and was one of some thirty-five such companies created by the state legislature between 1848 and 1873. W.J. Hutchins, the wealthy merchant who had declined the presidency of First National Bank in one of the early attempts to organize it, was the vice-president of the insurance company. Its president was B.A. Botts and its secretary, E.H. Cushing, owner-editor of the *Houston Telegraph.* Its other directors were prominent local businessmen, two like Cushing original stockholders of the Bank. Why the interests of these two concerns developed conflict and why their rivalry became bitter cannot be ascertained today, but the Bank survived it and the insurance company did not. It disappeared in 1886.

By fall the nephew, Fred Shepherd of Nashville, had joined the firm, but early in 1867 he was unable to conceal his disappointment. As Shepherd reported: "Fred is laid up with a cold. I don't think he likes Houston but he don't say so. It isn't Nashville but it suits me better." In April it was written to a New York correspondent that: "A month or so ago my nephew and partner announced to me that the climate and business did not suit him and he should leave here." Unwilling to continue the partnership enterprise without a member of his family to succeed him as principal, Shepherd stated, "Those who choose to deposit their money in a Bank managed by me may do so but I don't want to be individually responsible." Obviously he had opened merger conversations with his fellow directors of the national bank, for he and Wettermark did agree to take over its management. Another reason for his changed attitude he revealed in a letter of July 12: "On 1 July I proposed doing what may be a very foolish thing, as I have already intimated to you, to take into this office and with Mr. Wettermark to run the First National Bank of Houston . . . . I have $10,000 stock in the bank and Wettermark has $5,000—a little over 1/8th of the capital, but bad or careless management has caused its stock to be down and without some energetic management I suppose it will 'dry up.' When my nephew made up his mind to quit, I commenced thinking of this move. Now I see no better opened to me than to take hold of it."

During the balance of 1867, with Shepherd at the helm and Wettermark as cashier, weekly meetings of the board seemed to have contended solely with routine matters.

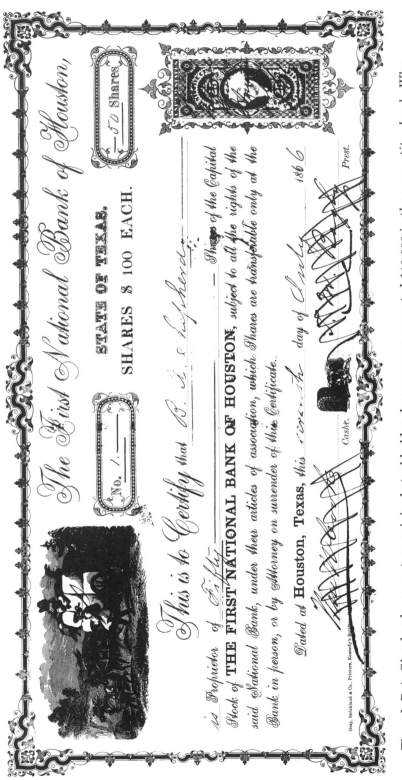

Though B.A. Shepherd was not an original stockholder, he very soon invested $10,000 in the competitor bank. Why he was issued stock certificate No. 1 is unexplained.

Because of a severe storm the directors did not meet on the regular day, August 28, and as a matter of fact, except for one session in September, they did not get together again until November 6. A yellow fever epidemic raged through the Houston area and the interior of the state, and citizens were afraid to congregate in groups, so Shepherd wrote. That summer and early fall it caused great distress and many deaths, particularly in the little towns along the railroads as far as 150 miles from Houston where the people were not prepared for it and fled terror-stricken in all directions.

Yet, in late September the Bank's president declared, "The Bank stock is worth par under the present management. Under the old it was not worth 80." With equal cockiness he reported to a brother in Virginia: "Am running the First National Bank of Houston. I have a good deal of its stock, and in this I expect to remain as long as I live. The salary and profits of the stock will handsomely support me." He might have known that there were problems ahead but he was certainly not prepared for an action taken against the Bank early in the following year. Neither did it occur to him that conditions might shake the strong confidence in Houston's business prospects that he had many times expressed.

Though it is not recorded in the minutes of the board, there is no doubt that the lease in the Pillot Building at Fannin and Congress authorized on May 1, 1867, was cancelled and the space never occupied, for as of July 1 the Bank was moved as a rent-paying tenant into Shepherd's bank building at Main and Congress. In January, 1869, the directors, acting in the absence of the president, agreed to ask the landlord for a reduction of rent but soon the answer came back in definite terms that the proposition would not be considered. Shepherd as landlord would not cooperate. It was not until April, 1870, that the board, following intermittent concern about improvement of the premises, with special emphasis on the safety of the bank's assets, made bold (this time in Shepherd's presence) to offer him $15,000 in gold for "the house and grounds now occupied." At the next meeting the cashier reported that the land owner was considering the offer, but the matter was never mentioned again. As a matter of fact, Shepherd decided to improve the safety factor

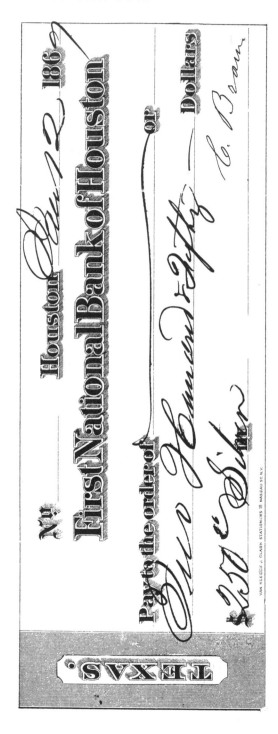

This early check called for payment in silver. Most deposits in 1867 were in gold or silver coin.

by building a new vault in the banking house. Then when the directors realized that the Bank's burglar-proof safe, once installed in Shepherd's vault, could not be removed, they proposed that he buy all the furniture, including the safe and some desks and some chairs, and this he did for $1,500, with an increase in rent thrown in.

Finally, in 1882, the Bank purchased the one-half lot and improvements on the southeast corner of Main at Franklin from Henry Brashear for $13,000. This was the same property for which they had offered A. Sessums $15,000 in gold in 1867. It had become known by then as "the old Cleveland corner," because William D. Cleveland, a young merchant and former employee of Sessums, had operated his business there following the failure in 1870 of A. Sessums and Company. Remodeling the one and one-half story brick building for banking cost almost $13,000, and after the bank had occupied the premises sometime in the summer of 1882 President Shepherd reminded the directors that certain desks and chairs transferred to the new quarters were, after all, his personal property. There was no contest, and he accepted $250 in settlement. It was at this location, gradually expanded and over the years improved and reimproved three times, that a First National Bank was operated until 1956 when it became, by merger, a partner in First City National Bank of Houston.

At the annual meeting of stockholders in January, 1868, the seven-man board of directors was again reduced in number—this time to five. An original stockholder, L.J. Latham, a former sea captain from Connecticut who had taken up residency in Houston in 1839, appears on the board for the first time. Except for two short periods his service as a director and later as vice-president also was to continue until his death in 1886. It was into the lap of this board that a bomb was tossed at the meeting of February 19, 1968. Shepherd reported that a suit for $10,000 had been filed personally against the Bank by Colonel B.F. McDonough, who was in his official capacity Assessor and Collector of Internal Revenue for the First District of Texas at Galveston. The colonel was at that very time advertising in the *Galveston News* his official demand that all persons owning cotton im-

This remodeled structure on Main and Franklin, the key business corner in Houston, was occupied by First National Bank from 1883-1904. The name in faint script can be seen on signs under the eaves and at the awning. Note the fruit stand against the wall on the side street. The tall building to the right contains the private bank of T.W. House and Company.

mediately render it for taxation at three cents a pound. The Bank was thus confronted by a politically formidable adversary, and the little paper of January 20, 1866, given him by Dr. Ingham S. Roberts proved, of course, to be the ground on which he based his claim.

Not one of those present had previously heard of this purported contract. It struck them all as a serious threat indeed for a little business operation just getting under way. Although President Shepherd had already been authorized to choose and employ an attorney should incidents arise requiring legal counsel, this was specifically so critical an issue that the directors, without hesitation, decided to call to the Bank's defense another original stockholder, the outstanding lawyer in Houston, Judge Peter W. Gray of Gray & Botts, predecessor firm to a succession of great firms, the present one being Baker & Botts. Nevertheless, the directors could not believe that McDonough could recover on so flimsy an agreement as that reflected in the paper given by Dr. Roberts two years before. After all, it was related to an entirely different effort to organize a national bank, the one dependent upon the willingness of William J. Hutchins to be president.

In the case of McDonough *vs.* First National Bank of Houston, Judge Gray won the verdict at a trial in the Third District Court of Harris County in its spring term of 1869. Later when the decision for the Bank was set aside by a higher court and the cause reinstated, he filed the defendant's answer in mid-March, 1870, and went through a second trial. It was not until that very month that he set his fee at $1,000 plus $500 should the matter reach the Supreme Court. As it turned out, this litigation remained in the courts until 1880, twelve years after the original filing, having survived six trials and four trips to the Supreme Court of Texas. The final judgment was against the Bank and its sureties, B.A. Shepherd and L.J. Latham, and was for $500 and costs, which speaks eloquently for the skill and tenacity with which the great Judge Gray more than earned his $1,500. Dr. Roberts' little informal memorandum given McDonough in January, 1866, under pressure to gain one day's time, had been sustained as a contract due compensation.

(62 H)   Houston Jany 20. 1866

B.F. McDonough /

We hereby agree to give
you by transfer Five Thousand Dollars
(in the stock of the First National Bank of
Houston when fully organized). As the
Sum of Five Thousand Dollars currency
whenever the Bank may be in operation
which shall be with as little delay as
possible. This is in consideration of expenditure
& services already rendered to the Institution —

Truly Yours B.F. Roberts

Com. 1st Nat Bank Houston

This "contract," given solely to gain one
day's delay, was the basis of a twelve year
suit for a "finder's fee."

At some point in the twelve years in the courts McDonough had assigned his interest to a W.D. Alexander, so it is not known how in the end he came out financially. Chances are he might not have fared as well as lesser figures. During the trials it had been brought out that Lorenzo Sherwood had been paid $4,000 and one G.W. Paschal in New York another sum. In court testimony, Muter Miller, deceased special agent, was shown as having on his trip to Washington and New York made these payments, probably without authority of the Bank's board.

The Bank had been assessed only a nominal penalty but during the long fight heavy court expense had accumulated. When President Shepherd made his final report to the directors on June 30, 1880, they expressed their approval and "in spite of enormous costs attending it (the suit), plus the legal fee of $1,500 to Gray & Botts, as well as the writing off of some items as bad debts," they declared a 6% dividend, the first of two such distributions for that year.

This long, drawn-out legal battle, which can be studied in thick packets of papers faithfully preserved in the files of the District Clerk of Harris County, called for testimony mostly by deposition from all the parties to all the efforts to organize a national bank in Houston. During one of the several trials of the case an interesting deposition was given in March, 1870, by H.F. Hurlburt, the Comptroller of the Currency after February, 1867, who was Deputy Comptroller under Hugh McCulloch when McDonough's application for a charter was filed in August, 1865. It sheds light on the casual way in which charter applications were then handled and valuable banking privileges granted. It is not surprising that political influence had its usual weight, but to have the Comptroller testify that "permission to organize a national bank was sometimes given verbally, in informal manner, and blanks given to the applicant" is revealing when compared to today's rigid standards. The act of providing an applicant with forms conferred, according to the Comptroller, only nominal priority and certainly no right that was saleable. Hurlburt further stated that "if, under such permission, a bank is organized, no further record is necessary. If one is not organized within a reasonable time, say a few months, the Comptroller of Currency is at liberty to consider another application from the locality if submitted by any other respectable and loyal citizens." Furthermore, "if it should appear that the applicant did not intend to organize a bank but did put forward other persons suitable to be entrusted with the forms, they doubtless would be recognized as applicants on their own merits while the original applicant would be ignored." Emphatically, the Comptroller dealt with the matter of compensation for original applicants transferring the forms to others. He declared it the policy of his office to deal with principals, not with agents or speculators; that if it had become known to him that McDonough was attempting to sell his permission it would have been revoked without ceremony.

In the minutes of a board meeting on June 18, 1868, when the Bank was barely two years old the first suggestion of financial loss appeared in a resolution "that the amount due by First National Bank of New Orleans written off in the last quarterly report be reversed so as to appear on the Bank's books in the original amount until its final settlement." In spite of it, the directors, confident that the McDonough claim would involve no loss, felt their little enterprise prosperous enough to warrant a 10% cash dividend, the first in a long history of generous treatment of stockholders. It was, however, June, 1872, before the second dividend was voted. Still supposed to meet weekly, the board is recorded as being in session only one more time during that year. On July 16 a brief meeting was held, not to transact business, of which there was apparently none, but to vote the president a leave of absence for sixty days, more or less. Presumably in Shepherd's absence 'the offerings" were to be considered informally by some of the others, but by this time the economic problems of reconstruction were being felt severely in Texas. Even though the state had escaped the burning and pillaging of war, only with the greatest difficulty were the crops planted and harvested, and a market center like Houston with about 9,000 population had little trade of any kind. By this time, Texas like the other Southern states had been put under military rule, and the Radical Reconstruction was soon to go into effect.

It was in this distressing atmosphere that stockholders of the First National Bank of Houston attended their annual meeting of January 12, 1869. After the usual formalities, the election of a chairman, the determination of a quorum, with 955 of the 1000 shares represented in person or by proxy, and the reading of the minutes of the 1868 Annual Meeting, Shepherd asked H.R. Percy to take the chair while he presented the following resolution: "Whereas, in view of the diminished commerce of Houston it is impracticable to continue profitably the operations of this bank, resolved that from and after the first day of April next, the same be placed in voluntary liquidation." Spirited debate ensued before the question was put and the result reflected by this minute: "Not receiving a 2/3 vote as required by law, the resolution was lost." Shepherd personally and as proxy for absent Director Speers, Cashier Wettermark, and two new stockholders, dry goods dealer Henry S. Fox of Houston, and Capt. J.J. Hendley of Galveston, voted a total of 624 shares in favor of dissolution. Directors Latham, Percy and Willis and former directors Brewster, Forsgard and Roberts, all original stockholders with faith in Houston, defeated the resolution with their 331 shares. Two of them, previously pledged to support Shepherd, had changed their minds and votes at the last minute. The infant bank had survived its first crisis. A switch of as few as 13 shares would have put it out of business.

The rejection of his motion was hard for President Shepherd to take. He had lined up the votes in advance and was shocked by the defections, for he wrote on February 18, 1869, to Speers, whose proxy he held, that having been "expecting to carry it (the motion) without doubt," he was now considering "selling out his stock to Henry Fox on an offer of $90 per share." The stock he said, "is bona fidely worth par and ought to continue to be if the Bank is properly managed by the folks. But, I am determined to get out of it if I can do so honorably without too much loss. And, if I do any more business in this town, I would do it on my own and have it entirely under my own control. I think Fox is acting as the 'tool' of Hutchins and the Insurance Company."

In March Shepherd reported to Speers that "in the matter of the bank stock, I don't suppose anything will be done now.

Since I wrote you Fox has sold out his $9,000 stock and re-signed as a director (he had been elected to the Board in January, just a few weeks before). I was in error in supposing he bid for mine for Hutchins. As I learned afterwards, he said it was for Runge and Company (an important mercantile firm in Galveston)." Fox may have had in mind only his own interests, for his operation as a merchant soon led him like others into private banking, and his success persuaded him in 1889 to found and head the Houston National Bank. Meanwhile, Shepherd was buying small blocks of stock at from 90 to 92½ and confided that "if I can get $8300 more I can put the concern in liquidation as I choose. Then I could defy them. I may yet surprise them one of these days if matters get too hot for me. I think by 1 July we may pay a 10% dividend and leave the stock worth intrinsically par, if no accident happens. But with all the fighting and opposition from the Insurance Company I see it will be hard work to do more than keep the stock at par value and pay 10% annual dividends. In this country where money is worth so much more, the stock will never sell for $100 which only pays that dividend."

Nevertheless, determination to gain voting control of the Bank drove Shepherd to buy any block of its stock whose owner he could persuade to sell. By April, 1869, he could report, "When at Galveston last I acquired the stock I needed to wind up the Bank if I elect to do so." Meanwhile, he admitted that "the Bank seems to have lost favor since I have been in it or else the commerce of the place is drying up . . . . The ship canal will hardly save it. In the canal I lack faith, do not see the necessity or practicability exactly and because I cannot seems to militate against my popularity here. . . . I am rather 'taboo' in the community because I could not regard it with favor."

The "ship canal," an idea that when first suggested in 1849 was to be accomplished by diverting the Brazos River into Buffalo Bayou, was one area of disagreement. It became an issue again in 1867 when a survey authorized by the city council proposed a channel from the foot of Main Street to Bolivar Roads. Shepherd's "friends on the other corner" helped organize the Buffalo Bayou Ship Channel Company to promote it and use it, but he took no stock in it. Forty odd years later the "canal" became a reality but its earliest champions did not, of course, live to see it.

In July, 1869, Shepherd wrote about the Bank, "Doing as well as can be expected for these dull times. As things stand now I don't know that I can do better than hold on. At least such are my present calculations. Do not wish my friends on the other corner (Houston Insurance Company—Hutchins, Cushing, *et al.*) to think they had any hand in expelling me from Houston if I do have to go." In August he followed with "The folks on the corner . . . caused a quotation to be inserted in the Telegraph of First National Bank at 91½. I knew that they held for Gray $2,000 for which I had repeatedly offered 95, so I concluded I would advertise thus—'Wanted— to purchase First National Bank stock for which will pay par notwithstanding it is quoted in the papers as worth only 91½.' So, the next morning as soon as the doors were opened, in popped Mr. Cushing with the $2,000 aforesaid for which I passed him a check very quietly and told him if he could find anymore at the same price to bring it in. The papers now quote it at par."

At the election of directors following the liquidation debate in the stockholders' meeting of 1869, President Shepherd and two of his supporters—his long-time partner Cashier Wettermark and Fox—represented the majority of the board, with Percy being re-elected along with Brewster, a former director, from the winning opposition. Within three months Fox and Brewster, one from each side of the issue, sold their shares of stock in the bank and resigned. They were replaced by Capt. Hendley and by Latham who appears to have led the fight against Shepherd's motion but to have gained his respect and a lifelong relationship. Considering how they had voted on the previous question of dissolution, the board with its two new members still contained opposing views. This was of no consequence, however, for liquidation, as the record shows, was never mentioned again in directors' meetings, that is, until sixty-four years later when First National Bank in Houston, "New Bank," came into being.

During the balance of 1869 "the depressed conditions of local finances" were more than once emphasized in the minutes of the directors and were reflected in their decisions on various minor problems. For instance, concern was expressed about delinquent notes due by the Houston and Texas Central Railway. The cashier was instructed to settle with H.&T.C. Railway by renewing the note of some $7,300 to be repaid in three installments due each thirty days thereafter. He did renew and obtained in addition the endorsement of W.R. Baker, one of the wealthiest men in town and a director of the railroad. A week later the Bank accepted for discount a $750 note of the company offered by a foundry to which it had been given. This evidence of confidence in the future of railroads must have been followed by other similar transactions, and in May the Bank received a reprimand from the authorities in Washington for extending credit to the Central in excess of the Bank's legal limit.

The H.&T.C. Railway, planned as early as 1852 to reach northwestward to the cotton growing areas of the middle Brazos River Valley and backed by Houston business leaders including B.A. Shepherd, had early construction and financial difficulties. But by 1861 when it was sold to W.J. Hutchins at a sheriff's sale, it had reached Millican, eighty miles away, having connected at Hempstead with the Washington County Railroad that crossed the Brazos and went through Chappell Hill to Brenham. New ownership and management found means to operate quite successfully during the Civil War years, and by the middle of 1866 they were actually able to report net profits from an increasing volume of traffic. Construction had, of course, been out of the question for at least five years, but in early 1867 work had been resumed on the extension of the road and by August rail service had reached Bryan twenty miles from Millican and two years later had been pushed through Hearne and Bremond to Groesbeck, one hundred twenty miles from Houston. The Central would grow in mileage and profits to become a major asset of the Southern Pacific System, but at times in the late '60s operating cash was obviously pretty thin.

Eighteen years later in 1888 another railroad which was to become a profitable part of the Southern Pacific System fell behind in its indebtedness to First National, and its notes for $3,099 had to be charged off. It was the Houston, East and

West Texas Railway which had been projected in 1876 toward the timber country of East Texas and into Nacogdoches before going into receivership in 1885, with foreclosure in 1892. It was another venture important to the development of the area which could not in its early years earn enough to pay back the cost of its construction but later blossomed out under new owners.

Upon his election to the presidency of the Bank, in connection with which a $10,000 salary had once been mentioned, Shepherd had presumably accepted as his annual salary the same $1,500 that had, in April, 1867, been voted his predecessor Bagby. By this time he had become the largest stockholder and was more concerned about the Bank's earnings than about his personal compensation. This seemed no time to increase the Bank's operating expenses, but in February, 1869, a committee appointed by the Board considered officers' salaries and recommended $6,000 a year for the president and $4,000 for Cashier Wettermark to be increased to $5,000 upon his return from a four-month trip to Europe for which leave of absence had been granted him. All this was duly approved. As it developed, Wettermark returned in three months and a Mr. F. Mohl, who with the title of assistant cashier had substituted for him, rented a vacant office above the bank for $50 a month and became one of Houston's early insurance agents.

The president meanwhile had begun a practice of reporting to the directors the loans and discounts made by him or by the cashier without prior reference. This meant by-passing the weekly meetings to "consider the offerings" and for a time such transactions already consummated were routinely approved. However, in July the directors raised a question about one borrower and voted that advances to him be confined to $1,000 and that "the President and Cashier were hereafter to conform." Less than a year later "margins (limits) were ordered to be spread on the record and observed in granting loans in the absence of the Board." This order referred to four lines of credit, one limited to $5,000, two to $1,000 each and one to as little as $500. President Shepherd was running the Bank, with or without a controlling interest, but the board was not to relinquish its authority, at least for the next few years. Later the infrequency of directors' meetings might suggest that a different policy had taken effect.

Toward the end of 1869 there began a succession of unusual problems apart from ordinary losses in the course of a money-lending business. Due to these problems, the stockholders, with expectations aroused by that 10% dividend when the bank was barely two years old, were forced to wait four years before receiving a second distribution from earnings. In November President Shepherd made this statement to the Board of Directors: "On September last I telegraphed to the National Park Bank (New York correspondent) using the following language—'Sell Thursday before noon $9,000 gold at 43⅝. Have $5,000 en route. Will make gold account good. Telegraph sale.' To this a reply was received on the 23rd: 'Sold $9,000 gold at 43⅝.' From that day up to October 28 the Bank had no information that the gold transaction was not a bona fide sale owing to the failure of the New York Gold Exchange without settling this obligation. So stated Mr. Kitchen, President, in his letter of the above date to the Bank. There is evidently a neglect on the part of National Park Bank in not notifying this bank sooner of the true position of the $9,000 gold and I do not see why the Bank should suffer for the bad faith of the third party with whom it is not connected. The Park Bank now offers the figure of 30% as a settlement but not being satisfied therewith I have referred the matter to S.M. Swenson, Esq., private banker in New York, soliciting his interest in our behalf to confer with the above named bank, agreeing to abide by his decision." The New York bank acting on the telegraphic instructions had sold the gold and delivered it, but the check accepted in payment could not be collected before the Gold Exchange failed. Why over a month elasped before this was reported to Houston cannot be explained. Nevertheless, the board fully approved of the president's action and ordered the statement placed on record.

The reaction of the directors was not surprising because S.M. Swenson was a personal friend of several of them and his reputation for integrity and sound judgment was well known to every businessman in Texas. Swenson, a Swedish immigrant who had worked two years in New York and

Baltimore, had been shipwrecked off Galveston in 1838 on his way to cast his lot with Texas. As years went by he amassed a considerable fortune as a planter in Brazoria County and in Fayette County. By 1850 he had followed the Capitol to Austin, engaging as merchant, banker, and large landholder. As an opponent of secession, he was persecuted and was forced in 1863 to flee to Mexico. On his way he stopped in Fayette County to have some brickwork done on a fireplace in his farmhouse there. The story is told that upon his return to the States at New Orleans in 1865 he sent a trusted friend to the Fayette County farm who, following instructions, dislodged some of the bricks in that fireplace and extracted $20,000 in gold. This gold delivered to Swenson enabled him to go into the mercantile business first in New Orleans and shortly thereafter in New York, where he was thus available to represent the Houston bank. That trusted friend who had recovered his capital and who was now turning to him for judgment was none other than B.A. Shepherd. There are many references to Swenson in the Shepherd papers, both before and after the Civil War.

Receiving this appeal, Swenson wasted no time in investigating the sale of $9,000 gold negotiated on order from the First National Bank of Houston and confirmed by National Park Bank of New York. Though it is not stated, the New York Gold Exchange through which the transaction was handled undoubtedly accepted delivery of the gold for an unnamed buyer and collapsed before settling the account. In any event, the National Park Bank under the cloak of its role as agent declined legal responsibility. Swenson reported to Shepherd that the New York bank had done its duty as agent and advised that the matter be pursued no further. So the board accepted the opinion of Swenson as final and ordered entries made to cover the loss. However, nobody was happy and the new board of directors elected in January, 1870, passed a resolution that since the position taken by the National Park Bank in the gold case was regarded as unsatisfactory, it was considered expedient to arrange with the National City Bank of New York to act as its correspondent.

In March, 1870, the failure of A. Sessums & Company occurred. According to an advertisement in the Houston *Directory* of that period, this was a Galveston house operating as cotton factors and general commerce merchants. Sessums himself lived in Houston and conducted a similar business in his personal name in the building at Main and Franklin that First National Bank had tried to buy from him in January, 1867. His reputation was excellent and the financial difficulties of his firm must have caught his creditors by the utmost surprise. As it was, the First National Bank had become involved not through their usual extension of credit but by innocent "purchase of exchange through the National Bank of Texas in Galveston in the sum of $25,000 gold." The Bank apparently had accepted a draft of A. Sessums & Company against its account in the Galveston bank which, when presented for payment, had been refused and protested. Every effort to ascertain extent of loss had been unsuccessful, for the stricken company refused to issue any statement of its condition. Rumor estimated liabilities in excess of assets to the tune of nearly $1 million, and the best settlement suggested to the creditors was 26¢ on the dollar, payable in four annual installments with 8% interest. This was indignantly voted down by the directors, and it was resolved to take legal steps. Yet a bit later on the advice of Director Hendley, a resident of Galveston, and after consultation with the bank's attorney, action in that direction was suspended.

The worrisome matter continued under negotiation, and with authority of the board the president agreed in June to a 25% settlement of principal and interest, accepted the cash, and surrendered the dishonored draft. A further consideration to the Bank was the promise of participation in certain life insurance policies issued by the Houston Insurance Company. The Sessums loss, so the stockholders were told at their 1871 meeting, had upset their hopes of the Bank's second dividend. At this time President Shepherd persuaded his associates to insert a Bank advertisement in the city's newspapers "for six months or longer." That sort of thing was not being done in those days. Nor was any advertising done again for a good many years. Indeed, some bankers considered it beneath their dignity to solicit business.

At the 1872 Annual Meeting President Shepherd proudly informed those present that the embarrassment to the Bank caused by the failure of A. Sessums & Company had been entirely overcome. Sessums had arranged that the Bank be protected by a participation in life insurance policies held by another institution. As it happened, Sessums died within two years and full collection was made then. It was reported at this meeting that an 18% surplus had accumulated in the profit and loss account, and that the directors to be elected would welcome a recommendation from the stockholders as to the payment of a dividend. Surprisingly, those stockholders preferred that the surplus be built up, in fact as soon as possible "made full according to the requirements of the law provided, however, that there shall be enough earnings for the current six months to make a 10% dividend by or before July 1st next." Business went so well that on June 20 the directors transferred $25,000 to Surplus and declared a dividend of 15%. In December there was another dividend of 10%. Thus began a series of annual or semiannual dividends that in a few poor years did not increase but in the long run grew steadily more generous.

Meanwhile, in 1872 another loss was sustained. This was a small one and not uncommon in the course of ordinary bank operation, yet it strained the relationship between First National Bank and one of its local competitors and the episode was considered worthy to be recorded in the minutes. Texas Bank and Insurance Company of Galveston had issued to an individual a check against its account with First National Bank of Houston. The check apparently made out for $2,000 was deposited in the City Bank of Houston and paid when presented to First National, the drawee. Later the Insurance Company discovered that what had been drawn for $20 had been raised to $2,000. It was immediately reimbursed for the overpayment by First National Bank, but when an attempt was made to recover from City Bank (no relation, of course, to a later bank with a similar name) under the usual implied guaranty of amount and endorsement, the answer was negative, "contrary to all legal decisions and precedent and analogous cases." First National Bank's only recourse was to retain attorneys in both Houston and Galveston and to permit no further exchanges of drafts with City Bank. Thirteen years later Houston's first clearing house for the local banks, then only two months old, recorded "the unfortunate occurrence of the suspension of City Bank," a polite way of taking note of the little state bank's failure.

Despite such occasional setbacks in the profit account, the Bank benefited from the growing commercial activities and even some industrial ones springing up in Texas despite several years of military rule. In fact, the point has been made that federal funds for subsidies, public works and U.S. Army payrolls more than offset the costs of state government imposed by federal troops. The crisis of 1873—a money shortage involving hoarding and runs on banks in New York and other centers and the failure of the Philadelphia firm of Jay Cooke & Co., financiers of the Civil War for the North—gripped the nation for five years but touched Texas only lightly. The planting and marketing of cotton and other agricultural products resurrected a healthy economy in the eastern part of the state while the delivery of cattle to out-of-state markets brought considerable wealth to all sections.

The Houston Cotton Exchange and Board of Trade was founded in 1874 and necessarily allied in the closest way to the local financial institutions. In 1885, soon after occupying its striking new building which still stands at Travis and Franklin Streets, the Exchange created a Committee on Banking and Insurance with Henry S. Fox, private banker, as chairman, and two others, A.P. Root of First National and Captain B.F. Weems of City Bank of Houston, as members of the five-man group. The committee's first act in August of that year was to add "a representative of the banking house of T.W. House, in order that the entire banking interests of the City shall be represented." In September the subject of a clearing house for Houston banks was discussed, and on October 2 a motion was unanimously approved to the effect that "A Clearing House be established in the City of Houston on and after October 15th under the management of E. Raphael (a real estate and insurance man, later appointed by William M. Rice an original trustee of Rice Institute). Said Clearing House to be located at the Houston Savings Bank, and the hour for clearances 'exclusively for currency' to be 2:30 p.m."

On October 5, 1890, "A meeting of the Banks and Bankers of the City of Houston, Texas, desirous of forming an

Association of Banks and for the establishment of a Clearing House was this day held at the Houston Cotton Exchange and the Board of Trade." Although using the facilities of the Exchange, the six banks of the city were actually breaking away from the Exchange's Committee on Banking and Insurance. They organized, with A.P. Root of First National as president and L.L. Jester of Houston National as secretary, formally arranged for their own clearing house, and turned its operation over to Raphael, this time as manager. Others present were R.A. Giraud of the Commercial National, J.E. McAshan of South Texas National, T.W. House of T.W. House and Co, and O.C. Drew of W.O. Ellis & Co.

From then on the daily clearings "in currency and in as large bills as practical" seemed to work well and without incident. Twice—on warning from the Secret Service Bureau of the U.S. Treasury of dangerous counterfeit bills in circulation—agreement was unanimous, once to rubber-stamp or steel-punch any such currency discovered, and once to accept $100 silver certificates for collection only. The first suggestion for joint action to protest the assessment of the banks for taxes was to appeal to the state comptroller to overrule the county tax assessor, but what luck was had is not recorded. The clearing house got a new constitution and bylaws in 1911, still with six members, the Union National and the Lumbermans National having taken the fifth and sixth places held in 1890 by the private banks and meanwhile by others that had blossomed and faded away.

At the request of Cashier Wettermark a special meeting of the board was held in early December, 1875. The record indicates no surprise when his resignation effective January, 1876, was submitted "in all friendship to the management and with the best wishes for the future prosperity of the Bank." He gave as his reasons "an unwilling duty to perform, as well as unpleasant, the present reduction of his salary and the uncertainty of future prospects." He had been a partner in Shepherd's private bank before and after the war and cashier of the bank for almost ten years, and Shepherd "unwillingly seconded" the motion to accept his decision.

In the 1870s there was a reasonable turnover of directors. H.R. Percy, a merchant and one of the original group, was regularly re-elected until 1875. Captain L.J. Latham, who had served for two years, 1868-70, came back on the board in 1871 and stayed until his death in 1886, serving a total of seventeen years. His record was far surpassed, however, by August Bering, a lumber dealer who was elected in 1876 and served for a stretch of thirty-two years. In the meantime, several businessmen had served short terms on the board followed in 1879 by two Shepherd sons-in-law, Alexander Porter Root, cashier of the Bank, and Owen Lynch Cochran, founder in 1856 of an insurance agency which still operates under his name. In 1886 Shepherd's only son, Frank, began a four-year term of service, and he was succeeded in 1890 by W.H. Palmer, a third son-in-law. Then, upon Palmer's death in 1902, W.S. Cochran, a grandson, was elected a director. When he retired in 1908, August Bering had been for a long time the only nonfamily member of the board.

Things had settled down to the point where for many years the directors were called upon to meet only three times a year. After their election at annual meetings of stockholders, which were rather perfunctory because one man owned a majority of the stock, the directors elected officers. They met again only to declare dividends, once in June and again in December, frequently of as much as 20% each six months. A few special requirements changed this routine, such as at the special meeting in 1885 to apply, with the concurrence of two-thirds of the outstanding shares, for an extension of the Bank's charter from February, 1886, to February, 1906, twenty years being the limit under the 1882 Act of Congress. The same procedure was followed in 1905 for another twenty-year extension. As president and majority stock holder, Shepherd ran a tight operation, and First National became generally known as "Shepherd's Bank." Indeed, by the end of 1875 he had accumulated over 80% of its stock.

The old gentleman, feeling the weight of his years, fifty of which were spent at hard labor in Texas (forty-five of them in Houston), chose the occasion of his 75th birthday on May 14, 1889, to express his gratitude to Houston for his good fortune as one of its citizens. To do so he set up a trust fund of $20,000 in city bonds with the income to be used for the "benefit of poor, indigent, and needy persons, who are now residing, or who may hereafter reside in the City of

First National Bank of Houston

35-1

Houston, Texas, _____ 19 _____

No.
216715

Pay to
the order of _____

$ _____

_____ In current funds

To National City Bank,

1-8 NEW YORK, N.Y.

_____ Cashier

American Bank Note Co.

It was not uncommon for nineteenth century banks to carry on cashier's checks and drafts the likeness of the president or principal owner. Mr. Shepherd's graced First National drafts far into the twentieth century.

Houston." (Able as he was in business, he so restricted the investment of the principal that after eighty-odd years it still remains at the original figure.) Besides his banking operations Shepherd had been deeply involved in most developments contributing to the economic growth of his community. Building construction, railroads, steamboat lines, even a textile mill, attracted him as investor and director. He served a term as alderman and put through a drainage ditch on Calhoun Avenue stretching from Louisiana Street eastward for miles into Brays Bayou. It was so far out of town as to get some notoriety as "Shepherd's Folly." The Volunteer Fire Companies and the Houston Light Guards were special interests of his.

According to the minutes of Directors Meetings, Shepherd presided as usual on June 30, 1891, but he was not shown to be present on December 31. By that time the capital structure had grown to $500,000 with deposits about $1.25 million. The seasoned old president who had headed the bank for twenty-four years had died on December 24, but not a word of notice nor of gratitude was recorded in the minute book. This was in keeping with his hard-nosed modesty but was definitely an oversight on the part of his associates. However, his death received proper attention in the community and was noteworthy for the statewide respect sincerely shown. The funeral was marred by heavy rains that caused mud so thick that the procession of carriages could go no farther than Franklin and Milam Streets. At that point the coffin, the family, and chief mourners had to be transferred to streetcars which took them out Washington Street to the gates of Glenwood Cemetery. From there they continued by foot through the mud for at least a quarter-mile. A substantial memorial to this pioneer is the Shepherd School of Music at Rice University, which was provided in the will of his granddaughter, Sallie Shepherd Perkins who died in Asheville, North Carolina in 1968.

"Shepherd's Bank" Turns Professional

In January, 1892, B.A. Shepherd's son-in-law number one, Alexander Porter Root, succeeded to the presidency of the Bank at a salary of $6,000 a year, the same figure named for the office in February, 1869. The vice-presidency went to son-in-law number two, O.L. Cochran, while son-in-law number three, W.H. Palmer, Assistant Cashier, was advanced to the cashiership. Mrs. Martha Elizabeth Roberts of Atlanta, Georgia, Shepherd's fourth daughter, was chosen to succeed her deceased father on the board of directors. The first meeting she attended was a special one in August, 1892, at which it was agreed to extend a loan of $20,000 to the City of Houston for six months with interest at 8% and "not less than $30,000 in bonds as collateral, provided the bank's attorney approve the validity thereof."

Root was born in June, 1840, in Georgetown, Delaware. His father, from Westfield, Massachusetts, had settled in Independence, Texas in 1838 and had married a Miss Mary Porter of Delaware who was visiting there. In order to have her first child at the home of her parents, young Mrs. Root made the round trip by stage and ship between Independence, Galveston, Wilmington and Georgetown. So the boy born in Delaware was brought back to Texas and grew up there. Attending Yale University and graduating in the class of 1861, he returned to the South to enter the

Confederate Army as a private. Serving in Texas and Louisiana, he was mustered out with the rank of major and joined his father in the furniture business in Galveston. In January, 1869, Alexander Root married the eldest daughter of B.A. Shepherd, and five years later he moved his family to Houston to be teller in the First National Bank, where he became an officer in 1876. Eventually his residence was established in the center of the block which was years later given by his children to become Root Square, a city park.

Owen Lynch Cochran, a native Tennesseean, was four years old when in 1838 his family sailed from New Orleans and landed in Texas at what is now Morgan's Point to settle

Bank president A.P. Root, left, discusses cattle business with a customer.

near where the San Jacinto River enters the Houston Ship Channel.

Within a year they had moved into Houston and lived in a tent for some time before a house was available. Cochran's first employment was as a clerk in the post office when he was eighteen. Soon he became an active member of the town's volunteer fire department and in the '50s was so seriously injured in a disastrous fire on lower Main Street that he was not later physically able to enroll in the military service. Instead, he acted as postmaster of Houston during the war years, afterwards becoming engaged in cotton brokerage until establishing Cochran's Insurance Agency in 1876. In that same year he married Shepherd's second daughter, Alice. In 1875 Cochran helped organize the Houston Land and Trust Company, now Houston Citizens Bank, and at his death in 1914 was its inactive president while holding the same position at First National. His son, William S. Cochran, had a distinguished career of fifty years with the First National and retired from the "New Bank" in 1947. He entered its employ as a messenger in 1898, became a director in 1902, an assistant cashier in 1904, cashier in 1908, and vice-president in 1918, an able ambassador for the institution. He was president of the Houston Chamber of Commerce in 1941-42.

On June 1, 1894, "Since the President and the Vice-President contemplated being absent from the City for some time, it was deemed advisable to elect an assistant cashier." John Thaddeus Scott was chosen, for the month of June only, to assist Cashier W.H. Palmer, Shepherd son-in-law number three. Over four years went by before he was made assistant cashier on a regular basis. However, so able he was in that role that in January, 1900, he was voted a bonus of $500 in appreciation of his "efficient services," and in 1901 he again received the same bonus plus a raise in salary from $2,400 to $3,000. The office of assistant cashier had first been used in 1884 for Frank T. Shepherd, who served for five years, and for Palmer for the year 1891 before his elevation to cashier.

The last decade of the nineteenth century opened with short-lived prosperity throughout the nation due to railroad building, good crops, and extravagant government expenditures for public works. But, there was the ever present uncertainty about the currency, all redeemable in gold, for which there was no fixed gold reserve. A period began when large amounts of currency were tendered for redemption and when the gold received went abroad or into hiding. The resulting currency shortage brought on a crisis in 1893. This was at the height of the long struggle in Congress for the inflationary authorization of free coinage of silver, the declining price of which had caused political difficulties in the mining states of the West. Tensions had been eased by the compromise Sherman Act of 1890 providing for additional but still limited purchase of silver by the Treasury. However, continued over-expansion across the nation brought on railroad receiverships, bank closings, and a weakening of confidence checked only by the repeal of the Act and gradually easier money. The silver fight continued with increasing force until the presidential election of 1896 sustained the maintenance of a gold standard for another thirty-seven years. Meanwhile Root, who had been president of First National for not quite two years, learned how to take care of the Bank's customers under conditions of money stringency, a lesson that proved very valuable in 1907, the last full year of Root's leadership.

For a number of reasons, such as the tragic Galveston storm of 1900 and the discovery of oil at Beaumont, the population of Houston grew rapidly as the twentieth century opened. It was obvious to President Root and his associates that the little one and one-half story building, once a wholesale grocery house, to which the bank had moved in 1883, had become wholly inadequate. In June, 1903, a key lot behind the old building, fronting fifty feet on Franklin Street and going back one hundred twenty-five feet, was purchased, and two lots at the Franklin and Fannin Street corner were leased for a temporary one-story structure on which work was started at once. By April, 1904, architects' plans had been put out for bids and a contract awarded for an eight-story bank and office building on an L-shaped steel frame allowing 8750 square feet per floor with twenty-five feet of frontage at the Main Street corner and one hundred fifty feet abutting Franklin. The winning bid was for $228,000 with completion in nine months. Banking operations were shifted to the temporary building, but by the middle of 1905 the new

This is a view of the banking room with mezzanine in 1902 showing employees John T. Scott in the foreground on the left and Fred A. Root seated on the right. Third from the left is George G. Timmins, fifth is William L. Porter, and sixth is W.S. Cochran. Second from the right is Frank E. Russell. It was in 1902 that Cashier Palmer had died while on a vacation trip.

The steel skeleton in the background is the beginning of the eight story building to be completed for First National Bank. A temporary building had been erected just behind at Fannin and Franklin Streets. The author, in sombrero, has just left the bank and is about to cross the streetcar tracks.

skyscraper was fully occupied. It was the first steel frame construction in Houston and took its place as one of the three tallest buildings in Texas, along with the Wilson Building in Dallas and the Wheat Building in Ft. Worth, both also eight stories high.

The temporary banking house and fixtures were soon put to use by a new bank, the Union Trust Company of Houston, later called Union Bank and Trust Company. It was the first bank chartered by the State Banking System authorized by constitutional amendment in 1904 and set up by the state legislature in 1905. Afterwards it erected and occupied for years in the name of Union National Bank the building now standing at 220 Main Street. Three years later in August, 1908, in the wake of the 1907 Panic, two neighboring buildings, each with twenty-five feet of Main Street frontage, came on the market and the First National bought them

An imposing new bank only twenty-five feet wide was completed in 1905. It still stands in 1975 as the northwest corner of the large building running along Franklin Street from Main Street to Fannin Street.

both for about $60,000 apiece. With the additional fifty feet in hand, the board decided at once to widen the too narrow facade of the banking building to seventy-five feet, and by year-end had contracted to spend some $200,000 more for the additional working space plus the seven upper stories for rent. This took care of all foreseeable requirements, although a small annex did have to be added to the rear in 1911.

A 1909 look southward on Main Street shows at the left work in progress to enlarge the narrow original building by fifty feet of new frontage. The steel frames in the distance are of the Scanlan Building at Preston Avenue and of the Goggan Building, now the inside fifty feet of the Bankers Mortgage Building.

The trying year of 1907 was a month old when President Root received authorization from the board to carry out his suggestion that each clerk be given "a check equivalent to one month's salary in appreciation for efficient service in 1906." Such a bonus was repeated in December, 1907, and thereafter became a Christmas tradition unbroken, as far as is known, to this day. In Houston—so removed from the great financial centers—there was little apprehension about the overextension of banks across the country. There had begun in the East a great increase in foreign and domestic trade and a tightening supply of capital and credit with which to finance it. This was accompanied by the inevitable trend to speculative excesses, and by the fourth quarter of 1907 metropolitan banks found themselves overextended. There were critical failures in New York, interior banks here and there were affected, the stock market slipped, confidence was seriously shaken, so there came the 1907 Panic.

Houston worked through the Panic bravely but not without anxiety and some distress. Currency and coin were scarce and had to be severely rationed. The use of checks was well established, so that transactions between business houses and their banks were not greatly impeded. But payrolls in that day were distributed almost entirely in cash, and the hardships due to its shortage fell heavily on the wage earner. *The Houston Post* reported November 18, 1907, that "the Houston Clearing House may authorize clearing house certificates in forms of scrip payable to bearer in $1.00 denominations to pass as legal tender." The resort to scrip did not help the laborer with many a corner grocer. First National Bank was highly liquid at the time, with its vaults comfortably filled with folding money and coin. It managed to meet the requirements of all its customers and to make some new friends, large and small.

Only one failure of a major downtown bank mars the city's twentieth century, that of the proud banking firm of T.W. House and Company, which was forced to suspend operations during the Panic of 1907. Founder T.W. House, one of the original stockholders in First National Bank, was a very early Houstonian whose bakery developed into general merchandise and eventually into credit dealings akin to banking. In time this latter became the more important activity, and when he died in 1881 T.W. House, Jr., his eldest son and business associate, bought out the other heirs and gave full time to the role of private banker. T.W. House and Co. stood for years "in the front rank of the responsible financial institutions in the State." Its 1907 rating for capital, never, of course, reported to any authority, was estimated at more than $1 million, with assets supposedly in excess of $2 million. Later in that year of financial stringency this private bank, like many banks across the nation, found itself unable to realize enough cash from its receivables to meet the demands of its depositors. It closed on October 17, 1907, and filed according to law a general assignment to a group of three outstanding citizens representing the creditors. It is understood that after many years of liquidation of miscellaneous properties full settlement was made.

Though the troubles of 1907 were of short duration they dramatized the need for banking reform, and Congress acted promptly in 1908 with the Aldrich-Vreeland Act, not only to provide additional currency in times of emergency but more important to create the National Monetary Commission of nine members from each House to investigate and present a program. After four years of study the Commission came up with a plan in early 1912, but action was delayed. With the Woodrow Wilson administration coming into power, the Commision's important findings were incorporated by Congress into the broader legislation of December, 1913, known as the Federal Reserve Act. Implementation was prompt indeed, and by the end of 1914 the Federal Reserve System was providing an elastic currency, a depository for member bank reserves, and facilities for short-term loans and for the rediscount of commercial paper. In April, 1915, the System's Eleventh Federal Reserve District in Dallas inaugurated as instructed an intradistrict plan for the clearing and collection of checks at par, and this in good time became part of a nationwide activity. Furthermore, a farsighted provision added to the Act retained the emergency currency authority of the Aldrich-Vreeland legislation, and that proved invaluable in cushioning the shock of the war exploding in Europe.

By mid-January, 1914, in response to a letter from Secretary of the Treasury W.G. McAdoo to all national banks, First National's directors resolved to accept the provisions of the Federal Reserve Act. In swift succession that year requisite shares of stock in the Federal Reserve Bank of Dallas were purchased, John T. Scott was named District Reserve Elector and soon he became one of the original directors. The application was made for membership in the National Currency Association under the Act; and as its share of the quota for Houston, a Reserve City, First National subscribed $150,000 to a gold fund for international exchange. After all this ready compliance, the Bank was honored by having to give up its able vice-president, Oscar Wells, to be the first governor of the Eleventh Federal Reserve District with residence in Dallas.

By August, 1914, First National Bank of Houston was one of the larger stockholders in the Federal Reserve Bank of Dallas, and it made application to be a depository of the United States government conditioned upon the pledging of eligible security in the required ratio. At almost the same day the Bank, upon admittance to the National Currency Association, increased its surplus account (to 20% of capital, or $400,000) in order to qualify. It was not until 1925 that it received designation as a Reserve Depository for funds of the state of Texas, also on a secured basis.

The spring of 1917 saw the United States enter the World War, and at once the nation's banks were called upon to cooperate with the Reserve Banks in the purchase of Treasury certificates and bonds for themselves and to help in their sales to others. When the first Liberty Loan was proposed in 1917, the Federal Reserve banks were designated the fiscal agents of the government, and member banks, both national and state, became for the duration of hostilities heavily involved in the distribution of bonds, war savings certificates and stamps. First National of Houston took its quotas in four Liberty loans and the Victory loan, meanwhile encouraging customers to buy and lending them money for the purpose. In addition, it participated by instalment subscription or outright gift, as all banks did, to Red Cross campaigns, war work campaigns, and to organizations doing essential work with service personnel. One novel and perhaps naive act of the directors in the period was to declare in June, 1917, a special cash dividend of 1/4th of 1% to provide funds that individual stockholders might voluntarily donate to the Red Cross. Much of this wartime activity would have represented problems without the unifying force of the Federal Reserve System. Banks have played the same roles ever since.

Beginning with Scott, a Mississippian who was hired as a bookkeeper in 1893 and was made assistant cashier in 1908, a succession of remarkable men were elected to senior positions in the First National. Through their influence, what had been "Shepherd's Bank" in the nineteenth century rapidly changed in the twentieth century into an institution with broader direction and management and diminishing Shepherd influence. As late as 1956 third and fourth generation descendants of the pioneer banker, a majority living in Houston but many scattered from coast to coast, probably represented as a group the ownership control of the Bank. However, the direction of the institution and the making of its policies had long since passed into the hands of career bankers—"professionals" if you please.

Most had backgrounds of sound banking experience and were called from outside to join the First National staff. The great Mr. Scott, however, moved steadily up the official ladder, to cashier in 1902, to vice-president in 1908, to president in 1914, and to chairman of the board in 1930. Then, for twelve more years, 1933 until his retirement in 1945, he was chairman of the "New Bank," First National Bank *in* Houston. But Scott was much more than a good banker. His citizenship made him one of the outstanding Houstonians of his time. A leader in the field of business directorships, of church affairs, of education in both public schools and in universities, of civic matters as different as the port commission and the art museum, he possessed the gentle qualities and concern for others that made him guide, counsellor, and friend for two generations of men and women. Scott had over the years received repeated invitations to senior management in very large banks in New York and other financial centers. In 1956, when the vaults of First National Bank in Houston were opened for the last time and the contents transported to the First City National Bank, the combination

John T. Scott worked in the Bank at every rank, beginning as a bookkeeper in 1893 and ending his active service in 1944 as Chairman of the Board. He remained Advisory Committee Chairman until his death in 1955.

of numbers to open the massive vault door had been for decades the date of Scott's birth, 10-10-1870.

Another important official who started with the Bank in 1890, and like W.S. Cochran as the lowest member of the staff, was Frank E. Russell, an outstanding Roman Catholic layman, a man of prodigious energy and industry with an unsurpassed talent for customer relations. He had served under Presidents Shepherd, Root, Cochran and Scott, had completed an invaluable ten-year term as cashier and director and was on the threshhold of even greater service as vice president when he died in early 1923 at the age of fifty-one.

In 1910 the president, O.L. Cochran, was inactive and the operation of the bank had become complex enough to demand a second vice-president to assist Scott, who was running the Bank as the only vice-president on the staff. Elected to that position was Herbert R. Eldridge, who had experience as a bank officer in Gainesville, Texas, in the Commercial National of Houston and in an important bank in Colorado Springs. Favorably known throughout Texas and active in the Texas Bankers Association, Eldridge proved an excellent choice in supporting Scott and in attracting valuable new business, especially from correspondent banks. He was so outstanding as to draw the attention of the National City Bank of New York, and he accepted a vice-presidency there in 1913. He advanced rapidly and was on bank business in South America when his heart failed in the high altitudes of the Andes. It was said that on the basis of his brilliant record in New York, had he lived, Eldridge would certainly have reached a very high position in the National City Bank.

At the annual meeting of stockholders in January, 1913, the six-member board of directors was increased to seven. The large stockholding of Mrs. W.H. Palmer, daughter of Shepherd, was obviously entitled to representation. Her son, Edward A. Palmer, had worked in the Bank from the time of his graduation from college and had in January, 1908, been made an assistant cashier and a director, but he tragically drowned that very summer. So her son-in-law, an experienced cotton exporter, Edwin L. Neville, who would later be an active senior officer in the "New Bank," was elected to the directorship. Eldridge's resignation had created a vacancy which logically was allotted to his successor, Oscar Wells, the new vice-president already chosen for that responsibility. He was an urbane professional of thirty-eight with fifteen years of experience as an officer of six banks, three in his native state of Missouri and three in Texas. In fact, he had served in two Houston banks just across the street and was to last less than two years with First National. Seasoned in the practice and theory of banking, he was an admirable choice to be the first governor of the Federal Reserve Bank of Dallas which opened in the fall of 1914. But, he was essentially a commercial banker and in early 1915 accepted the presidency of First National Bank of Birmingham, Alabama, becoming chairman of the board in 1930, a position he held until his death in 1953. Wells had become an outstanding business leader in Birmingham. In 1925 he served as president of the American Bankers Association, in that role just nine years ahead of the man who succeeded him at First National of Houston.

The Bank had been so wisely selective and successful in bringing in talent that its new vice-presidents were too often called too soon to broader spheres of action. For the third time in four years it found itself seeking a senior officer. During this period, inactive President Cochran had died, Scott had moved up to the presidency, and W.S. Cochran had become a vice-president. Again a vacancy had to be filled, preferably with a man with a state-wide reputation among bankers, hopefully one who could, as Eldridge and Wells had done, hold correspondent bank business and bring in more like it. Francis Marion Law, cashier of the First National Bank of Beaumont, seemed to fit the special qualifications. He had worked up in the banking business, beginning as a bookkeeper and as an assistant cashier in Bryan, gaining rich experience in three banks, and he had been happily involved in district meetings and conventions for Texas bankers. He was invited to Houston for an interview with Scott. Making a favorable impression, he was offered and accepted the job, and then the question of salary came up. Law's top salary up to that time had been $300 a month, so when Scott mentioned $7,500 a year, Law blurted out, "Why, Mr. Scott, I am not worth that much money!" To this came Scott's reply, "Young man, if you are not worth $7,500, you are not the man we want!" That settled it. He reported for duty as a vice-president in January, 1915.

Law made a place for himself without delay, soon moving up to senior vice-president and to president in 1930. After World War II, when P.P. Butler came from the presidency of the American National Bank of Beaumont to become president of First National in Houston, Law was elevated to chairman of the board and even after his retirement remained as consultation chairman, later at First City National as well. Meanwhile, he had participated in the political activities of the banking profession in Texas and later in those of the nation, so that in 1924 he had been elected president of the Tex-

Francis Marion Law, successively vice president, president and chairman of the Bank from 1915 to 1955, was president of the American Bankers Association, 1933-1934.

as Bankers Association and in 1933 president of the American Bankers Association. Law was a forceful and entertaining speaker and a public-spirited citizen of the first rank. His longtime chairmanship of the Board of Directors of Texas Agricultural and Mechanical University was the most prominent activity of a broad range of involvement in public and civic causes to which he gave energy, judgment and leadership.

Chosen the president of the American Bankers Association for a year beginning in the autumn of 1933, Law accepted the challenge and responsibility of reestablishing communications with the White House. President Roosevelt, in the anxiety of his first few days in office when the whole financial structure of the nation was about to collapse, was properly critical of some bankers and alienated most of them, especially those on Wall Street, in his reference to "money changers in the temple." As a "country banker," one who headed an institution just reorganized, Law had few friends in the big New York City banks, but one of them—Seward Prosser, chairman of the board of Bankers Trust Company—was willing to set up a luncheon for him with the heads of the leading New York banks. The atmosphere was hostile, and Law's proposal to convey to the President an offer of cooperation was greeted with disdain and disapproval. Yet, after bitter debate a willingness to try was arrived at, and with that sort of grudging support Law approached his appointment in Washington. President Roosevelt was slow to believe that his enemies would suggest peace, but the ice was broken and gradually it became possible for Law and the A.B.A. to help in the drafting of the important banking legislation which Congress passed in the wake of the Depression. In the fall of 1934 at the annual convention of the A.B.A. in Washington, it was Law's privilege as out-going presiding officer to present President Roosevelt for the principal address and to hear an arch-conservative banker, Jackson Reynolds of the First National Bank of New York, make a gracious conciliatory response.

Before World War I banking as a profession in Texas continued to hold an attraction for able young men needing basic exposure to business before deciding upon a permanent vocation. It was not uncommon for college graduates to go to work as runners or messengers for banks, and some liked the business well enough to stick. Returning veterans of 1918, however, saw brighter prospects in other lines such as the developing oil industry and manufacturing. Nevertheless, in the '20s First National was fortunate enough to add to its staff some outstanding men, some of the best of whom had no college background. Chief among these was Sam R. Lawder, vice-president and director, who served twenty-one years before accepting in 1944 the presidency of a major competitor, and M.D. Jenkins, with some forty-five years service from assistant cashier to retirement as senior vice-president and director. Both of these men were Federal Reserve trained. Others deserving mention, all starting from the bottom, were H.R. Eldridge, Jr. (1917-1956), W.A. Kirkland

(1920-1963), and L.H. Thomas (1926-1969). More remarkable for success from a modest beginning was A.E. Cleere (1919-1970), who was employed out of primary school, rose through all the operating ranks to become senior vice-president with executive duties of every type, and who upon retirement was elected active president of a successful neighborhood bank. The problems of 1932 brought Dewitt T. Ray to First National in January from an automobile dealership where he had been an office manager though with prior banking experience. Ray was first employed as manager of the First National Company, an affiliate. Soon he was assistant trust officer and then rapidly moved into general executive duties, finally to vice-president and director before leaving in mid-1943 to become president of the Liberty State Bank of Dallas; later he was vice-chairman of the Republic National Bank there. In 1946-1947 he was president of the Texas Bankers Association.

In 1942 an investment man, Thomas Watt Gregory, Jr., came into the New Bank as vice-president and director, and until his retirement made an important and distinctive contribution to its growth and profit. After the unexpected losses in 1944 of both Ray and Lawder, First National again went to a neighboring city for a seasoned vice-president, this time Perkins P. Butler, president of the American National Bank of Beaumont, who accepted election with the understanding that he soon be made president. So, in January, 1945, this personable and energetic leader began a memorable thirteen-year term of constructive banking leadership. Finally, as chairman, Butler together with Kirkland who succeeded him as president, led in urging the decision to move the institution, accomplishing it by merger, eight blocks south into the new downtown business center.

In the years after World War I, banks began tentative steps to broaden their services. First National led in many banking innovations but was slow to offer interest on time deposits until competition made it advisable to open a savings department in 1922. Vice-president H.R. Eldridge, when he became a director in 1910, had seen to it that customers were given the opportunity to earn interest on idle funds through purchase of certificates of deposit ("restricted as far as possible to 3% for six months or more, with 4% allowed only in extenuating circumstances"). The C.D. business was never solicited or advertised, and consideration for the small saver had been postponed a good many years. Large accounts, in many cases representing the "extenuating circumstances," were benefited at the time by the payment of interest on daily balances, an expensive practice that was debarred in the new banking regulations of the '30s. In the lending field, First National made a new departure in banking by the rediscounting of installment notes secured by chattel mortgages on automobiles. That was after World War I and long before the appearance of finance companies handling all types of time-payment paper.

First National Bank pioneered for Houston in the foreign trade field in 1922, first by subscription to stock of the Federal International Banking Company of New Orleans, established by law and under Federal Reserve regulation, and second, over two years later when that agency liquidated, by setting up its own foreign department with an experienced officer brought in to run it. Cotton shipments from the Port of Houston had long been handled by drafts on foreign purchasers, accompanied by ocean bills of lading, which had to be routed through New York banks as bills of exchange or acceptances. The growing volume of exports of increasing diversity eventually called for direct dealings with the banks of the importing nations.

For decades trust business in Texas did not apparently seem compatible with commercial banking operations and know-how, and First National invariably recommended that fiduciary matters, wills, trusts, guardianships, and the like be taken up with the Houston Land and Trust Company. It was a friendly institution across the street which had no banking privilege and was not a competitor. Later developments and the establishment of full service trust companies in Houston seemed to require that each big bank have a trust department of its own. So in January, 1927, First National was granted trust powers and directed two of its regular officers to give part-time attention to it. Closer supervision and expert administration by an able chief clerk carried it through to more formal status in the New Bank under D.T. Ray, trust officer, and L.H. Thomas, assistant, who was to become a vice-president and senior trust officer.

As has proven to be the case in every decade of the twentieth century, Houston's growth and the increasing pressure on facilities of all kinds have out-stripped advance planning. By 1920 First National's lobby and other spaces were again outmoded. Fortunately, the property on the corner of Franklin and Fannin Streets which was temporarily leased in 1904 had been acquired in 1918. It was determined to double the existing eight-story structure, to renovate the banking quarters, and to project the lobby and tellers' counters straight through from Main Street to Fannin Street. A contract was awarded in May, 1923, and within a year the Bank had moved into the new half, the old part had been remodelled to match, and the eventual opening of the whole revealed a magnificent banking room with mezzanine, adequate supporting spaces, vaults and other facilities, all of which were still modern and efficient in 1956 when the "New Bank" entered into merger and moved to the newer business center of Houston.

Jubilation over the prospect of a new banking house was in the same May of 1923 shattered by the discovery of a forgery that could have meant the heaviest loss in the Bank's history. The managing partner of a cotton shipping firm of good reputation had for years borrowed for his company against cotton awaiting shipment. At that time the firm was using credit to the extent of approximately $400,000 secured by the pledge of a warehouse receipt for 4086 bales of cotton. By accident the Bank learned that the borrower had little cotton stored in the particular warehouse, and a close inspection of the receipt showed that it had been raised from 86 bales to 4086 bales. A silent partner came forward to the extent of his means, the forger went to prison, the Bank sustained a heavy loss, and the one-bale cotton warehouse receipt became thenceforth the standard unit of this banking procedure.

Over the years, changes in the Bank's capital structure had from time to time become necessary and advisable, usually in connection with an expansion program. After forty years of operation the capital remained $100,000, and despite a liberal dividend policy, surplus had amassed in the amount

The First National Bank building as it was in 1956 before the merger with the City National Bank. Enlarged three times in fifty years, and expanded by purchase of adjoining buildings, its plant occupied over one-half block.

of $500,000 plus considerable undivided profits. In June, 1906, a 400% cash dividend was declared payable out of surplus, available solely for the immediate purchase of $400,000 in new capital stock. This was, of course, a stock dividend

A view from Main Street to Fannin Street with the officers' platform in the foreground to the right.

but, long before the imposition of income taxes, could be handled on a cash basis. In January, 1909, after employing a half-million dollar capital for less than three years, stockholders needed to double it to a million dollars by dividend of $300,000 from surplus and by outside cash subscription for $200,000, another "stock" dividend on a cash basis, but only a partial one. The same general method was used for a third time in February, 1912, when capital was doubled again, adding another million dollars by cash dividend of $300,000, all to be spent for new shares, plus $700,000 to be received from the sale of new stock, with prior rights to stockholders. It was not until June, 1923, that an increase in capital was accomplished by the method in use today, an offer of 5,000 new shares, pro rata to stockholders, at $150 per share. This action increased the capital to $2,500,000 and added $250,000 to surplus.

The First National Bank of Houston had traditionally been a liberal lender and a staunch foul-weather friend. It had grown and prospered and regularly paid healthy dividends, but it was not without experience with disappointing credits and losses to be charged off. Its early records reflect the necessity of taking over land to satisfy unpaid debts. In May, 1923, the First National Company was organized for the purpose of relieving the Bank of "Other Real Estate," an account which had built up to almost $200,000 as the result of settlements and foreclosures. Stockholders of the Bank were given prior rights to subscribe to shares in the company, and those not readily exercised by some Shepherd heirs were sold to others. The contract between the parties required the company to pay $150,000 for an option, to be exercised in whole or in part in twelve months, to buy real estate from the Bank at the supposedly low value at which it was carried on the Bank's books, but with any profit from subsequent sales of the land to be divided equally. The payment was made, many purchases completed, and the company disposed of several properties and shared the benefits, if any. Finally, in the late '40s when the company was debt free and inactive, it seemed best to liquidate its remaining assets of land and of oil, gas, and sulphur royalties. The stockholders exercised their rights to receive pro rata interests in either type of asset or in a combination of both, all set up in a trust handled by a neighbor bank.

However, the city was entering a period of rapid growth. In fact, the city grew at a rate of over 100 percent in the decade from 1920 to 1930, and the volume of banking activity, deposits, loans, and earnings swelled proportionately. First National's trusting credit policy and generous dividends prevented retention of earnings in amounts adequate for the building of surplus, which would later be sorely needed for distressing times no one foresaw. The stock market crash of 1929 was portent enough, and as early as the summer of 1931 the supervisory authorities began to question those policies and to urge the infusion of new money into capital and surplus. So, in September, 1931, 5000 new shares at $200 each were offered to the stockholders. Most of the controlling shareholders paid for their proportionate parts, leaving a relatively few shares of stock to be sold to new investors. Unfortunately, a dramatic local bank crisis developed almost immediately that autumn, and it required costly contributions from all Clearing House banks to rescue two troubled institutions. This fell heavily on First National.

The crisis started at 7 o'clock on Sunday morning, October 25, 1931, when William C. Costello, secretary to Jesse H. Jones, hurried downtown in response to a summons an hour before to find his employer seated behind his desk, hat on head, the odor and residue of many cigars suggesting an all-night conference. The supposition is that at least one desperate group, that representing Public National Bank and Trust Company of Houston, had been appealing to him for help.

Costello was instructed to call together for an important confidential meeting the heads of all the downtown banks. They met at the Jones office on the thirty-third floor of the Gulf Building at 2 o'clock that very Sunday afternoon, and no one left the well-guarded place until 5 o'clock Monday morning. Sandwiches and coffee had been sent in, and the analyzing and the planning and the tiresome argument with doubters droned on, with more than one of those present taking short naps on the floor with folded coats as pillows. A second session began late Monday afternoon, and that, too, extended through until the following dawn. This session included a carefully selected number of professional men and business leaders. In fact, it had been estimated that more than fifty men took part in these tense meetings of which no hint leaked out in those forty critical hours. Today not one of them survives.

From the moment on Sunday when the key bankers were informed that two banks, Public National and one other, might not open on Monday morning, it was understood by all that the failure of two institutions would, after two years of economic depression in the land, so undermine local public confidence that heavy withdrawals of deposits would put extreme pressure on the others, no matter how sound. The president of one of the smaller banks took the position that if its depositors should become panicky and start a run, he would voluntarily close his institution rather than allow some to withdraw their funds at the expense of others. He was persuaded to stand firm when, after hours of argument and counterargument, it was agreed that in the event of trouble the strong banks would jointly support the little ones for the Monday to follow. Then the weary conferees adjourned at 5 a.m. that Monday, went home to change clothes, and returned downtown to their banks. Meanwhile, committees of hard-nosed lending officers had been appointed with instructions to make secret examinations and appraisals of the assets of each bank for a report Monday night.

The business day on Monday passed without a run or hint of one, but the bankers gathered again at Jones' office and with the additional business leaders spent another night. The question now was how to prop up two weak members of the Houston clearing house, and at once a sharp division developed. Some expressed definite refusal to lend direct aid or credit to mismanaged competitors. When one man threatened to jump from a window, another stepped over and opened it for him! He didn't jump. In that atmosphere a late hour long-distance call by Jones to a venerable chairman of the board on vacation in Massachusetts converted his vigorously dissenting bank president in attendance at the meeting, and it was finally agreed by all that it was too dangerous to the people of Houston and their economy not to provide major financial support, and at once. By mid-night the examining committee reported that the two ailing banks could be saved only by the sale of one of them to strong ownership and by cash contributions of $1,250,000 for the rescue of the other.

Arguments continued at length. First, as the feelings cleared somewhat, the control of the older bank had passed into experienced and wealthy hands with $800,000 of its slow and marginally secured notes removed by refinancing. This was a credit set up on a long-time secured basis to be divided among the other members of the clearing-house. Next, the Public National Bank and Trust Company had been merged into the National Bank of Commerce, which received the $1,250,000 supplied by the other banks and several major corporations as protection against loss in assuming the deposit liabilities of the failing institution. First National Bank of Houston took a $200,000 participation in the refinancing package and paid in $150,000 cash as its part of the indemnity fund. These were tidy sums for an institution with problems of its own secretly gnawing at its vitals. By dawn Tuesday, October 27, 1931, the job was done, and that day's morning paper, purposely delayed in the printing, carried the news of the action that protected Houston from serious banking disaster.

Serious trouble for Houston had been averted, but after contributing so heavily to the rescue operation and charging off additional losses, First National had little left of the $1,000,000 new surplus provided by the sale of stock only a few weeks before. The cushion counted upon to carry the Bank through further trouble was shrinking dangerously. By May, 1932, it became obvious that for the protection of depositors something more and substantial had to be done to bolster the Bank's capital.

To relieve the pressure on the bank further, Mrs. Martha Elizabeth Roberts, last surviving daughter of Mr. Shepherd, Mrs. E.L. Neville and Mrs. E.A. Peden, two granddaughters joined by their husbands, also John S. and W.S. Cochran, two grandsons, plus some great-grandsons and granddaughters, and several senior officers contributed stocks and lands to a new corporation, The Statex Company. These gifts were used as collateral to support a $1,000,000 note of Statex given to the Bank in purchase of an equal amount of slow receivables and other doubtful assets. One of the granddaughters, the Bank's largest stockholder, accounted for almost half of the individual sacrifices for the defense of the institution.

Again, as late as March 11, 1933, in the middle of the Bank Holiday, more repair work was done in preparation for the reopening of Old Bank along with other banking institutions of the country rated solvent or important enough to survive. The overriding purpose was to buy time so that Old Bank might be adequately reorganized.

Rescue Job

Looking back upon the gradual deterioration of bank assets that began with the Stock Market crash of October, 1929, and led inexorably to the Bank Holiday of March, 1933, it is possible to identify policies and practices responsible for bank failures and for the reorganizations of banks that could not be allowed to fail. Well into the twentieth century many bankers were still extending and servicing loans without the aid of up-to-date credit information, including personal financial statements. There was still the prideful dependence upon the character, the family background and the generally accepted business standing of the borrower to be given excessive weight in the lenders' decisions.

Later, when loans became subject to doubt and criticism, lenders were slow to press collections before it was too late, and many definitely refused to sell out old customers whose stocks and other collateral were declining in value almost too rapidly for such action. There was blind faith in people and in the recovery of their assets. All these attitudes were commendable but far too risky in the light of responsibility to depositors. Furthermore, as the painful shrinkage of asset values continued, such a policy proved a positive disservice to the borrower whom the lender mistakenly thought he was helping. Better to be sold out with the loan paid and the balance, if any, available in cash than to be carried to the bottom with a debt still outstanding and the value of collateral depending entirely on hope of recovery.

Typical comments from an examiner's report of late 1930 indicate the conditions that were increasingly apparent in the Bills Receivable account of many a city bank. "There is an excess of slow and doubtful paper, a large amount of which is past due. As a result of current economic conditions there has been a definite decline in value of the security pledged, particularly local stocks against which the advances have been too large. Corporate and especially foreign bond issues are not proper investments for a bank's portfolio." A capable deputy comptroller to whom the above report was made might have sent to the particular bank involved the following injunction. "The examiner advises that your bank has been able up to now to operate successfully on a liberal credit basis. Now, however, conditions are such that the best interests of the Bank and its depositors demand operation along the most conservative lines, and especially should your loan policy be protective and your collection policy continuously energetic."

By the same token, when credit losses were reducing the undivided profits account and absorbing current earnings too, all banks were under pressure to reduce overhead and embrace every possible economy. The service charge on small accounts was the prime topic of discussion whenever bank operating men chanced to meet. It obviously was designed to eliminate the unprofitable accounts and to produce a new source of revenue from the marginal ones that remained. First National, always a champion of small business and the individual, followed the trend with great reluctance and instituted the charge in October, 1932. It was at least two years behind the times, if judged by the practices of other banks of the period.

As the '30s opened with the markets in trouble and business shrinking, the value of bank assets and the dependability of local credits continued to decline. The Reconstruction Finance Corporation just established by the United States Congress had begun in 1932 to put out banking fires in stricken cities, but withdrawals of deposits and individual hoarding accelerated to such an extent that banks throughout the country came to realize that they could not meet the demands upon them. Banks began to close in all states, and beginning as early as October, 1932, one governor after another declared a banking moratorium for his state. By Inaugural Day on March 4, 1933, Governor Lehman had found it necessary to close the banks of New York State. Realizing that hardly a bank in the nation was open for business, Franklin Delano Roosevelt moved to grasp the critical banking situation as soon as he took the oath as President of the United States. Two days later he issued an executive order to set up the incredible "Bank Holiday." In a "fireside chat" a few days thereafter, he declared that the temporary moratorium would end for all sound banks—first those in reserve cities, then banks in cities with clearing houses, and then other banks—a group a day for three days beginning March 13. The emphasis in this decree was that only *sound* banks would be allowed to reopen. Every bank in Houston, a reserve city, stood the test, and all resumed active business on that first day.

After the Holiday First National Bank had reopened for business but its directors still had doubts about its future, and they determined that a major repair job was essential to protect all parties as well as the business climate of the city. They went to the Reconstruction Finance Corporation for help in designing and financing a reorganization plan. This was worked out after weeks of careful study by officers of the R.F.C. acting on appraisals and recommendations by Chief National Bank Examiner, R.H. Collier, of the Eleventh Federal Reserve District, and his able and dedicated first Assistant, W.A. Sandlin. Bank president Francis Marion Law spent a month in Washington to keep in close touch with the office of the Honorable J.F.T. O'Connor, Comptroller of the Currency, who with his associates was kept closely informed by the excellent bank examiners in Dallas. In its design, in its working, and in its results, the plan proved unique. No other bank reorganization has been comparable to it in concept, execution, or final triumph.

Pursuant to agreement with the authorities, the Bank's Board of Directors resolved as of May 1, 1933, that "because of existing economic conditions and their adverse effect on affairs of this bank it has among its assets various items of uncertain and indeterminate realizable value and other items conceded to be losses, which assets amount in the aggregate to a sum approximating the capital stock, surplus, and undivided profits of this bank" and that "it is the judgment of the directors that it is manifestly to the interest of its stockholders and to the Houston business interests and more especially to the depositors of this bank to liquidate its affairs under a plan that will insure full protection to said depositors."

The reorganization procedure was put into operation on the morning of May 3, with its several steps thoroughly outlined in advance and accomplished at exactly the same moment. The purpose of the plan was to provide the entire capital of a successor bank, First National Bank *in* Houston, or "New Bank," for which a charter was being sought. To do so, First National Bank *of* Houston, "Old Bank," borrowed $3.74 million from R.F.C. and reloaned the funds in full at $125 a share to seventeen of its officers and directors. As security to the R.F.C. for its loan, the "Old Bank" going into liquidation pledged all its property not transferred to the "New Bank," its doubtful bills receivable, bonds and investment, other real estate and miscellaneous assets of every character, plus most important of all, the stockholders' notes totaling $3.74 million. Behind these notes, of course, had been assigned all of the shares that the new stockholders had bought, 100% of those outstanding except for eighty qualifying shares, of which each of the eight duly elected directors had acquired ten for $1,250 in cash. Miscellaneous collateral pledged to R.F.C. was valued at $4.145 million which, when added to the stockholder's notes of $3.74 million, built up a total of $7.885 million. With the entire capital structure thus subscribed and paid for on the basis of $3 million of capital, $600,000 of surplus, and $150,000 of undivided profits, a charter was granted and the First National Bank in Houston, "New Bank," opened its doors to the public.

From the very first, the seventeen borrowers, being all of the stockholders of the "New Bank," used their stock, exclusive of the eighty unpledged shares of the directors, as collateral to notes in favor of the "Old Bank." They agreed among themselves that they were acting as trustees for the stockholders of the "Old Bank," although they were under no legal obligation to do so. These men and women—whose traditions, careers, and fortunes were wholly involved in the "Old Bank"—had such faith in its recuperative powers after a financial transfusion and a slight change of name that they assumed those heavy obligations in the depths of a depression of uncertain term. Each had lost or had committed every eligible asset and now themselves as well—without the slightest thought of personal gain at the expense of others.

At the close of its first day's business on May 3, 1933, the "New Bank" found itself with deposits of $28 million, loans of $14 million, a bond account of $4 million, and cash of $14 million. It was for 1933 a clean, going concern with inherited earning power producing from the start. Despite the shock of its birth, a solid public confidence and good will immediately proved its richest assets. Its predecessor, First National Bank of Houston, had at the end of 1931 reached a deposit high of $41 million, but in the troubled year of 1932 this had shrunk to $34 million and in early 1933 the shrinkage had understandably continued. Indeed, the "New Bank" lost $1 million of its opening deposits within its first three weeks. Then the trend reversed and by the end of December, 1933, there was a reported net gain in deposits of $5 million to make a total of $33 million, including a growing $7 million from correspondent banks. From then on deposit growth was slow and steady.

Beginning with the first dividend distributed November 3, 1933, six months after the "New Bank's" opening, all dividends issued for the following eight years were distributed subject to a resolution of the Board of Directors passed on that same date. This resolution required that dividends be applied first to the payment of accrued interest on the stockholders' notes and the balance, if any, be passed to the "Old Bank" to be held in reserve for future interest payments on its debt, "it being the sense of the directors that the R.F.C. should obtain the benefit of all of this dividend" and of all following ones.

As the economy of the nation struggled to right itself in the middle '30s, the wheels of industry picked up speed, jobs opened for the millions of unemployed, and signs of improved purchasing power appeared. The banks of the country performed their routine functions and cautiously extended credit that was being cautiously sought, but they were severely blamed for failing to curb the speculative excesses of the '20s and were used as whipping boys by populist politicians. Banking reform was high on the congressional agenda, and new legislation, some of Republican origin, was pushed through both houses by the Democratic administration just returned to power. First came the establishment, as provided by the Glass-Steagall Banking Bill of June, 1933, of the Federal Deposit Insurance Corporation to guarantee the safety of the first $2,500 of each bank customer's deposit. By the same Banking Act of 1933, the payment of interest on daily deposits was forbidden. This was a boon to banks and so was the elimination of double liability on their common stock, a feature that had impeded the raising of new capital. Another important 1933 provision, not recorded in the Bank's minutes because it was applicable in only three or four major banking centers, was the separation of investment banking from commercial or deposit banking.

To qualify for F.D.I.C. insurance of deposits by the deadline, January 1, 1934, banks had to show resources adequate to offset their deposit liability, and many needed additional capital at a time when their common stock could not be marketed. The R.F.C. had been given authority to buy from banks preferred stock, debentures, or capital notes, and this proved the only source of needed strength for the hundreds of institutions that were undercapitalized. Some 2000 such banks found at year end 1933 to be on the borderline of adequacy were certified as solvent and insurable with the understanding that capital would be bolstered at once. Within six months all had been supplied with the required additional strength—from local sources and from the R.F.C. Nevertheless, there was reluctance by banks to issue preferred stock for sale to the R.F.C. They feared such an act might be construed an admission of weakness, and this situation was not helped by the patronizing aloofness of those banks who were already, or thought themselves so, adequately capitalized and liquid.

The chairman of the Reconstruction Finance Corporation was Jesse H. Jones of Houston, an outstanding public servant who had been director general of the Military Relief for the American Red Cross in World War I, a banker and city-builder at home. He was later to become Federal Loan Administrator overseeing Federal Housing, Home Owners Loan Corporation, Export Import Bank, and finally Secretary of Commerce with World War II responsibility for Metals Reserve Corporation, Rubber Reserve Corporation and Defense Plant Corporation. He was not a man to be thwarted and he took a personal hand in making preferred stock a must for most banks, using the tremendous power of his office and organization to pressure leading banks across the country, particularly in New York, to set strong examples by selling preferred stock to the R.F.C. even though a few did not themselves need it. More than 6000 banks strengthened their capital structures by this means, some retired their preferred stock within the first year, and within ten years a very high percentage of the others had redeemed their preferred stock out of earnings and loan loss recoveries without diminishing their resources.

In March, 1934, First National in Houston sold $2.5 million in preferred stock to the R.F.C., almost doubling its lending capacity. Thus it was capable of extending or participating in much larger prime credits, especially in the oil industry, with obvious improvement in earning power. In this case preferred stock proved a most advantageous liability and in a bit over ten years it had, entirely from retained earnings, been replaced by new capital and retired.

Pursuant to a clause in the Banking Act of 1935, notice was given in March of that year that the privilege, accorded national banks in the 1864 legislation, of issuing their own bank notes would become inactive. The procedure used was to call for redemption by July 1 all government bonds eligible to be lodged with the Treasury as security for such issues of notes. These securities included the ones specifically designated for that purpose, namely the famous 2% Consols of 1870 reissued in 1930 and the 2% Panama Canal bonds, plus U.S. Government obligations carrying a rate of not over 3⅜% which had been made temporarily eligible in 1932. It will be remembered that in early 1866 before the little new First National received its charter, it had under pressure waived the valuable circulation privilege accorded national banks, but that seven months later a special emissary to Washington City had managed to regain it. From then on First National had from time to time of its own volition given up that privilege and later reapplied for it. By the turn of the century, however, issuance of its own national bank notes had become an established practice and remained so.

Today, years later, the Depression is history, but in 1933 climbing out of its depths was grim business that took imaginative new leadership in Washington, both executive and legislative, working valiantly together to dispel the blackest clouds and to re-establish hope. Nevertheless, once "the fear of fear itself" was cast aside, the people of the U.S. felt their strength and confidence returning and set about to rebuild their economy. Markets stabilized and values of possessions, real and personal, began to recover. The government threw its resources into the battle, and, though mistakes were made, the overall assistance of the R.F.C. and other emergency agencies was constructive from the beginning and almost wholly effective. Congress did approve economic, fiscal and monetary measures, some of dubious long-range value, but the private enterprise system and the resilience of the American people were the prime elements in a recovery that gained momentum steadily, despite one or more setbacks, until with the advent of World War II depression disappeared.

It was at this period that the oil industry, entering its modern phase just before 1930, began to reach a new plateau in exploration, discovery, and production. Scientific techniques applied to oil finding, to improving drilling equipment, and to extracting products from crude oil opened vast new opportunities for profit and service to society and the economy. The great East Texas oil field was the most important of many major discoveries in the '30s, but its rapid extension brought about for a time quite unhappy consequences. Its broad productive area of small land holdings was drilled to an unrestricted density of wells, made possible by the low cost of reaching oil sand at a relatively shallow depth. For a considerable period the swiftly increasing production under no regulation built up a volume of oil above ground for which there were no adequate storage facilities. Long trains of tank cars could not transport it fast enough. The market for crude oil at the well was glutted, and the price structure collapsed. On the ground of wanton waste of an irreplaceable natural resource, both state and federal governments became involved. Despite strong political opposition in Austin and Washington, and determined non-compliance in the field, sometimes mixed with violence, restriction of production by proration of each oil field and of the existing wells in those fields, plus reasonable limitation of permits for additional drilling, became the law in Texas. Almost simultaneously such control gained the backing of federal legislation sponsored by U.S. Senator Tom Connally of Texas. It spread gradually in the name of conservation to the other oil-producing states.

There quickly developed a body of oil and gas law governing such conservation principles as proration of production at the wellhead and improved spacing standards. This latter included, since the courts had long since recognized their necessity, offset wells to prevent drainage of subsurface oil by wells on adjoining leases. Such dependable controls restricted overproduction, thereby stabilizing crude oil prices and making it safe for commercial banks to lend money to the owners and operators of producing leases where the volume of oil in place could with reasonable accuracy be certified by geologists. Oil in the ground is legally part of the realty so that the same recordable deed of trust instruments used in land mortgage banking plus enforceable assignments of the monthly production and its sales proceeds were the means used to provide security for bank loans. This type of loan payable with interest in monthly installments proved simple, safe, and self-liquidating. With modifications to fit special situations and income tax complexities, it became the basis for billions of dollars of sound financing, short term and long term. It is not surprising that an urgent demand for oil banking of this sort soon confronted Texas and Oklahoma banks.

Cities involved in the East Texas oil field had traditionally been included within the Dallas trade area, so it was natural that independent oilmen developing leases in that field should go to Dallas banks with their financial problems. Similarly, those operators in the newly discovered fields in South Texas gravitated toward San Antonio. Banks in both cities pioneered in the business of lending against oil in the ground, and soon banks in other Texas centers learned how to serve customers in like fashion. First National Bank in Houston (the "New Bank") made its first conventional oil loan in mid-1934 and proceeded to develop the first oil lending department in its community.

From the time in 1901 when the Spindletop Field in Beaumont came in, the "Old Bank" had handled the bank accounts of individuals, partnerships and corporations engaged in the oil business. That included, of course, extending credit to worthy borrowers to use in developing oil properties. Indeed, there still persists a tradition passed along by John T. Scott, who later became chairman, but was assistant cashier at the time that a critical loan was made to the newly formed Texas Company, possibly in connection with its exercise late in 1902 of an invaluable option on leases at Sour Lake. Another such story is related by Francis Marion Law, who in January 1915 resigned his post in Beaumont to become a vice-president of First National Bank of Houston. Barely settled in his new position in an unfamiliar town, Law was approached at his desk by three oil men, R.L. Blaffer, W.S. Farish, and Ed Prather, who needed to send $50,000 to Burkburnett, Texas, by noon the same day to nail down a promising lease. In great haste, they requested a loan of that amount. Personal financial statements were not customary in those days and none was mentioned. Law explained that President Scott and Vice-President Cochran were out of town, that he was new on the job and had never made a loan of that size, that the applicants were obviously businessmen of substance and standing but were strangers to him, and that he would appreciate being given an hour's time. Before the hour was up, he telephoned the gentlemen, advanced the funds to them, had the money transferred to a bank in Burkburnett, and received confirmation that the lease transaction had been closed. This property proved so productive that it was a major asset of the Humble Oil and Refining Company when it was founded in 1917 by those three along with several others. Law had called a key director, E.A. Peden, to his aid. Peden, knowing well the characters and abilities of the borrowers, encouraged him to make the loan and agreed to share the responsibility. This young vice-president was almost afraid to tell the president upon his return, but did so and learned happily that Scott would have done exactly the same thing.

Though learning new ways to serve the petroleum industry, First National Bank in Houston was not entirely without experience in that field and was proud, particularly so soon after its reorganization, to be chosen to participate in the dramatic sale and purchase of a highly successful Texas independent oil company. On July 31, 1935, when the bank's total deposits were something over $41 million, a single deposit of almost $42 million was made by a new customer-for-a-day, the Stanolind Oil and Gas Company of Tulsa, Oklahoma, soon to be Pan American Petroleum Corporation, and now Amoco. The funds were placed in the Bank that morning to be paid to Wright Morrow of Houston in purchase of assets of Yount-Lee Oil Company of Beaumont. The assets were to be acquired by Morrow through liquidation of the company stock, 100% of which the stockholders had agreed to sell him for over $45 million dollars. To make up the difference between his payment to the Yount-Lee stockholders and what he would receive from his sale to Stanolind, Morrow needed a bank loan to supplement the substantial cash account coming to him in liquidation of the company. First National's agreed lending limit was only $300,000, but its chief New York correspondent, National City Bank, joined it in a $1.8 million loan secured by valuable assets of Yount-Lee not included in the Stanolind sale. So, in the name of Morrow himself the Bank held on deposit for that day a large additional sum. By nightfall the funds in the new accounts of Stanolind and of Morrow, which had more than doubled the Bank's deposits for the day, had been paid out, but most of the money remained on the Bank's books in the names of the individuals who had sold their Yount-Lee stock or in Beaumont banks for their accounts. Deposits at the close on July 31 were $83 million and a day later were still $71 million. Though the proceeds of the sale were grad-

This check was drawn against a deposit that for one day doubled the Bank's total deposits.

ually transferred or invested, a healthy amount stayed on deposit for a long time, and after that red letter occasion the "New Bank" grew steadily in volume of business and profits.

The prospective transactions between the owners of Yount-Lee Oil Company, Wright Morrow as middle man, and Stanolind Oil and Gas Company had been through negotiation and evaluation stages for at least a year beforehand. Though the amounts involved were of record size for that day, it was the well designed and executed tax-wise manner in which they were closed that accentuated the drama of the event. In the Director's Room of First National Bank in Houston all the stockholders and their attorneys met with senior officers and attorneys for Stanolind. That important third party was also present, Wright Morrow of Houston, with his lawyers and tax consultants.

Carefully rehearsed, the closing proceedings directed by Chairman of the Board A.W. Peake of Stanolind unfolded in three stages, with checks and documents involved at each stage being placed for a few hours in the hands of a vice-president of the Bank acting as "stakeholder." First, Morrow, signifying his willingness and ability to buy all the outstanding shares of Yount-Lee, presented checks made payable to each seller, and these were endorsed and passed to the stakeholder. Simultaneously, each seller delivered to the stakeholder corresponding stock certificates properly assigned to the buyer by executed stock powers.

Second, Morrow, now conditional owner of 100% of Yount-Lee stock, had the shares transferred to himself on the company's books except for one share each to two associates, and all these shares were also placed in custody. Then, accepting the resignation of all officers and directors of Yount-Lee, Morrow in on-the-spot meetings had new directors and officers elected, and minutes later they caused the Yount-Lee Company to be placed in liquidation. At this point all assets of the dissolving company were transferred to Morrow as liquidating dividends in cash and in kind. Here again, all resolutions, stock certificates, conveyances and checks for Yount-Lee cash were put in the hands of the stakeholder.

Third, transfers and conveyances of oil properties from Morrow to Stanolind plus checks to establish certain escrows for known and unknown contingencies were given by Morrow to the stakeholder, while the officials of Stanolind did their offsetting part by putting in his custody checks on the Bank payable to Morrow for the purchase price of those properties.

Finally, it was possible to report to the assembly that there was on hand and in balance all items necessary to complete each stage of the sale successively, and therefore to attain the end objective. Up to this point, if any participant, seller, middle man, or buyer, had found cause to withdraw from the complex transaction, it would have been possible to call the whole business off, and the stakeholder could have easily undone each stage by returning in reverse order all items deposited with him. In this way all parties would have been restored to their original positions just as if no conditional exchange of assets had taken place. Now, the "Master of Ceremonies," Peake, having put the question and determined that no objection was to be voiced, directed the stakeholder to distribute to the proper recipients all the properties in his custody—checks to the sellers, Yount-Lee assets to the middle man, oil leases, pipelines, etc. to the buyer.

Successfully explained in advance to the Internal Revenue Service and given tentative approval, the procedures were planned in this order to incur the minimum in income tax liabilities, and they proved to be both ingenious and effective. The Yount-Lee Oil Company disappeared with honor and with none but its ordinary income taxes, its stockholders were accountable for their normal capital gains, the middle man, Morrow, established his base cost and presumably only after he had been able to recover that cost from the disposition of all Yount-Lee assets received in the liquidation distribution, that is cash, oil properties, real estate, listed stock, receivables, etc., did his tax liability begin to accrue.

It was over ten years later, in the postwar '40s, that another tax-saving method of selling oil properties was designed and put to use in many major transactions. This was the A.B.C. plan, involving an oil payment purchaser plus a seller and a buyer dealing for a producing property subject to the oil payment lien on a high percentage of its future production.

Since its opening in 1933, the "New Bank" had operated with only eight directors, all senior officers at work every day. This had certain advantages but they were outweighed by disadvantages, and in January, 1938, Chairman Scott told the stockholders in annual meeting that consideration should be given to the election of some nonbanker directors, men to bring sound, outside business judgment to the policy discussions of the Board. No action was taken on this feeler or on reminders presented to stockholders for successive years that the location of the banking house was no longer in the more active business district. Indeed, it was not until the stockholders meeting of 1942 that the suggestion for relocation was dignified by inclusion in the minutes and it did not show up again for five years.

The outbreak in Europe of World War II immediately alerted Houston's industrial establishment, and banks including First National got early lessons in the financing of defense contracts. All this became very real after December 7, 1941, and problems of personnel were soon added to those of banking participation in the war effort. Four of the Bank's officers were given leaves of absence in early 1942 to enter military service, and a third of the male employees gave way to female replacements as they resigned to enlist. The Bank and its remaining people began a four-year involvement in all-out effort for war production, for concern for service men and women, and for the care and relief of their families.

But—what had become of the First National Bank of Houston, Old Bank, that had gone out of business on May 2, 1933? Its liquidation had proceeded under Otis W. Jackson as liquidating agent. Jackson had been an employee and an officer of First National Bank of Houston for many years and was its cashier when in 1929 he had resigned to become vice-president of Guardian Trust Company of Houston. An able man of unquestioned integrity, he became providentially for all concerned available in mid-1933 and threw his sagacity and old familiarity with First National credits into the orderly collection from the Old Bank's assets of funds with which to reduce its $3.74 million debt.

Almost at once, with the recovery of the nation's economy, and with the close cooperation of the growing New Bank, assets of the Old Bank began to come alive and collectible. By the end of 1936, less than three years after its demise, over half of the R.F.C. debt had been paid. Liquidation proceeded more slowly after that, and by December 31, 1939, $900,000 remained to be paid. Finally, in October, 1941, after some eight years, the Old Bank reached the end of its obligation, originally $3.74 million. The assets of doubtful value left with it when in May, 1933, the New Bank took over its good business had by wise handling produced the wherewithal to discharge that indebtedness with interest. Old Bank still owned many items of more or less realizable value, but its chief and vital asset was that package of individual notes of fifteen heroic stockholders of the New Bank, being all the original group except two whose shares had been turned in upon their deaths and their notes cancelled. Those notes still held by the Old Bank totaled $3,525,900, secured by 28,207 of the 30,000 shares of New Bank stock. But the stockholders, each a note-signer, had by unwritten agreement been acting as de facto trustees for the owners of the stock of Old Bank. So they surrendered their New Bank shares in exchange for their notes, and as the end of 1941 approached, First National Bank of Houston, Old Bank, still in liquidation but debt-free, found itself holder of over 90% of the outstanding shares of First National Bank in Houston, New Bank.

Finally, two days before Christmas, 1941, the stockholders of Old Bank received the reward for their patience. They had, many of them unknowingly, faced in 1933 the total loss of their investment in the Bank, plus the threat of assessment of an additional $100 per share under the double liability of bank shareholders then part of national banking law. For almost nine years they had, of course, received no dividends from an institution undergoing liquidation. Now assembled at a called meeting, they took the last steps in the original plan of reorganization by voting themselves a liquidating dividend of ninety-four shares of stock of New Bank for each one hundred shares of Old Bank owned, with settlement for fractional shares on the basis of $175 per share. Their old stock, once valueless and assessable, had through the recovery of values following the Depression, been restored to a sound value of $164.50 (94% of market at $175) per share, now nonassessable. Furthermore, they voted to deliver to the New Bank in consideration of its assumption of all liabilities or claims against their Old Bank (none outstanding but income taxes) all assets remaining in the liquidation, some $250,000 in good notes, securities, and real estate, plus $40,000 in receivables rated 'fair' and other items of indeterminate value. This meant the end of Old Bank and the cancellation of National Bank Charter No. 1644 that bore the date of March 22, 1866.

At this enthusiastic meeting full restitution was made and warm tribute was paid "to that small group of large stockholders who in the year 1933 voluntarily pledged and mortgaged their properties in order to tide the bank over the crisis then existing." Then it was noted that "no officer in the bank traded in the bank's stock during the eight years notwithstanding the obvious opportunity for profit." In closing, President Francis Marion Law quoted the Honorable Preston Delano, Comptroller of the Currency, as saying, "Yours is the best recovery of any bank reorganization assisted by this office. Tell your people that their record of liquidation has been the best in the United States." There is the very strong presumption that the plan of reorganization of First National Bank of Houston, under the supervision of the Comptroller and his staff in the Eleventh Federal Reserve District and with the imaginative and practical financial help of Reconstruction Finance Corporation, was in all respects the only one of its kind.

New Vigor,
New Team

The war year of 1943 was a difficult one, and when the stockholders met in 1944, two vice-presidents and directors out of the eight senior officers on duty had resigned to take presidencies in other banks. There appeared to be no junior men ready for promotion to those key posts, and directors were authorized to select and employ a leading banker from some other city. The two glaring vacancies on so small a directorate as First National's, composed solely of active officers, called for a reversal of policy to allow for the election of outside directors in the future. To the six held over from the 1943 Board there were added in 1944 five able businessmen: John H. Crooker, a lawyer; J.W. Evans, a cotton exporter; J.H. Kurth, Jr., with lumber interests; W.A. Sherman, cotton seed oil manufacturer; and George Sawtelle, independent oil executive. From there on for the twelve years of the life of the New Bank, except for four active officers who became directors in the course of a merger, only two were elected to the Board from the Bank's staff.

When Mr. P.P. Butler, a man with all the needed qualifications, came over from Beaumont and took office as of May 1, 1944, in the position of Executive Vice President, it was, as reported, with the understanding that he would become president in 1945. Butler wasted no time in assuming a share of active responsibility and leadership, and after election to the presidency spearheaded constructive measures such as a pension plan, a parking garage, building improvement, a 25% stock dividend, and better operations and forward planning. His foresight and impetus to First National's growth was significant in negotiations toward a merger with the State National Bank of Houston.

A good neighbor of First National, the State National Bank since 1925 had occupied its own attractive banking house and office building at 412 Main Street, between Preston and Prairie. Organized by John A. Wilkins and his brother, Horace M. Wilkins, in June, 1915, as State Bank & Trust Company with $100,000 capital and with five employees, it had operated successfully around the corner at 912 Preston and had been granted a national charter in 1921. It had enjoyed experienced and progressive management, an admirable staff, and a small board of business and professional men as directors. In exactly thirty years, an original investment of $10,000 plus two exercises of rights for $7,500, or a total investment of $17,500 to purchase 175 shares at $100 par value, had grown to 5,000 shares of $20 par with a market value of $175,000. This was all solid enhancement arising out of profitable banking of high standards that earned the respect and good will of the public.

An opportunity was presented to First National in March, 1946, to receive this growing institution into partnership on terms worthy of its history and excellent personnel. After due approval by the stockholders of both banks, a merger was consummated in May which proved to be congenial and mutually advantageous. State National brought excellent individual and commercial accounts to the New Bank, and some outstanding trust business as well. No abler officers ever helped to run First National than the Wilkins brothers who served until retirement, John A. as vice-chairman, Horace M. as executive vice-president, and J.M. Jackson, vice-president and head of the trust department until his unexpected death in May, 1952. Henry Oliver, vice-president who joined First National with the same title, soon became a valuable member of the strong banking team and was a ranking senior vice-president when he retired in 1971. All of these men became from the date of merger directors of the

Bank and active members of the policy-making executive committee of First National.

Immediately after World War II long deferred housing construction in Houston set a pace that has seldom slackened in almost three decades. As the city limits were pushed out in all directions, large shopping centers were developed and with them came the demand for neighborhood banking. State law contained a provision for the affiliation of two banks, and downtown institutions began to use that means to extend their influence into outlying markets. The City National Bank had been the first in Houston to see its possibilities, having affiliated with Harrisburg National and Heights State in the early '40s. This relatively young bank founded in 1924 by James A. Elkins as Guaranty Trust Co. had absorbed the Gulf State Bank in 1928 and emerged as City Bank and Trust Company. Nationalized in 1934, it grew rapidly and soundly, and by 1947 when it built for its banking house the first multistoried structure in Houston following the War, it had become an important competitor for the increasing new business of the Greater Houston area.

In mid-1946 First National Bank realized itself a bit late in reaching out to the neighborhood centers. It jumped into action only to make the mistake of organizing three stockholders groups to apply for three separate state bank charters at exactly the same time. Two competing banks were alert enough to take notice, and each supported the filing of an application, one each for two of the areas chosen by First National. The solution reached by Banking Commissioner L.S. Johnson and his board was inevitably to award one charter each to an applicant backed by one of the three banks. Two applicants organizing with First National's help were badly disappointed, but the one promoting the Port City State Bank received its charter and managed to open by October, 1946. Control of the Industrial State Bank, a going concern on the east side of the city, had been purchased by stockholders of First National and an affiliation established in July, and in the following year of 1947 the Fidelity Trust Company near the Cotton Exchange was brought into affiliation as Fidelity Bank and Trust Company. These three relationships proved mutually advantageous and profitable.

At the same time downtown banks better situated than First National—from six to eight blocks southward on Main Street—were aggressively capitalizing on their strategic locations at the hub of downtown business activity and were growing at a much faster rate than First National. By 1951 National Bank of Commerce had taken first place in Houston with its deposit total, and by 1953 City National had become the second largest.

The year 1947 began for the Bank's stockholders with enthusiastic acknowledgment of the beneficial results of the merger accomplished seven months before. Nevertheless, there was persistent discussion of the necessity of abandoning because of outmoded location a banking house that appeared to meet almost every other requirement for efficient operation and satisfactory service to customers. A decision to move at once could not be agreed upon, so the alternative was to improve as fully as possible the attractiveness of the existing plant, banking rooms, and rentable space alike. On Main Street a more inviting entrance was provided. On Fannin Street a well-planned parking garage for customers and tenants was built, and by 1950 the sprawling eight-story building, erected by stages in 1905, 1908, and 1923, was successfully air-conditioned throughout.

The keynote of the postwar years was aggressive competition with fast growing banks six and seven blocks south where downtown business was by then concentrated. The first imperative was to maintain close customer relationships and the cordial lobby atmosphere traditional with this institution. Special staffs were created for the solicitation of new business, local, areawide, and national, with emphasis too on superior attention to correspondent banks. Nor was the effort neglected to explore additional types of lending, broader opportunities for sound, constructive credit extension in conventional and new directions. These included among others, term loans, mortgage warehousing, assigned accounts receivable loans, and installment loans, unsecured or secured by chattel mortgages. Furthermore, greater emphasis was placed on expansion and development of the trust department. This was undertaken promptly by State National's vice president, J.M. Jackson, upon the transfer of his excellent trust business into First National. Its importance was highlighted after Jackson's untimely death by Butler's success in persuading Carroll D. Simmons, vice-chairman of University of Texas for Business and Finance, to succeed him as head of that division. All of these efforts brought returns in growth and in profits, but not enough to satisfy an interested and ambitious board of directors nor the responsible officers either. Change of location had to be the prime consideration if First National Bank were to regain its accustomed leadership in total deposits.

In early 1953 a committee reported inability to identify a suitable Main Street site which could be purchased. A few months later a promising merger was discussed, appraised, and later abandoned by joint decision of both parties. A year later the site committee spoke of a key half-block available for $11 million for which no enthusiasm was expressed, and at the end of 1954 another merger possibility was ruled out. When in January, 1955, President Butler was advanced to the chairmanship after his tenth year, his successor Kirkland, who had long advocated the major change, pledged himself to give top priority to its accomplishment by buying land and breaking ground for a new building.

Such planning and maneuvering proved to proceed with frustrating slowness in 1955. Meanwhile, it was decided to assume the offensive, or to put on a bold front, by buying for apparent expansion for drive-in facilities and the like, the land and two buildings adjoining, with 125 feet on Main Street. One building next door, a very old structure on a forty-foot frontage, was razed and the site graded and landscaped. The other, with a handsome banking facade abandoned by a competitor quicker to move, was put to use for overflowing departments, and in fact served well for such a purpose until 1961. Today it is owned and for a time was occupied by United Fund.

Preparations for action on the overriding task included an increase of capital stock approved by the Bank's stockholders in April, 1955. It took the forms of a stock dividend of two shares for every fifteen held and of the offering, readily subscribed at $40 each, of three additional shares for every seventeen. Next was the employment of a local professional and an out-of-town man especially experienced in congested urban centers to undertake a comprehensive survey of adequate building sites. Their reports, ably analyzing a number of locations, centered upon one on which a verbal option was then taken. When duly reported to the directors this met with almost unanimous approval. However, as the time approached for final decision on the posting of earnest money for the purchase and for the selection of an architect, a thoughtful minority of the Board made these points: one, that the city and its business establishment badly needed a big bank, one in size roughly comparable to each of two banks in the rival city of Dallas; two, that four of Houston's sizeable banks had modern banking facilities in prime locations and that the addition of another plant, however up-to-date, would not correct the city's competitive disadvantage; and third, that the principle of merger had so much to offer that it should be explored one more time. A change of course was then taken and a merger committee of five appointed.

This was mid-November in 1955, and for the next four weeks the merger committee covered much ground. It reported at the December directors' meeting that there appeared to be the possibility of a combination with either of two banks, both of size comparable to the First National, each with excellent quarters and room for expansion. The directive to the committee was to continue negotiations until it could recommend the prospective partner with which an agreement of greatest advantage to First National stockholders could be reached. Early in January the committee reported to a special meeting of First National directors that a merger with the City National Bank of Houston seemed to be the most desirable and that the terms tentatively framed were fair to the stockholders of both institutions. The directors agreed, they authorized the signing of an understanding between the executives of the two banks, and ten days later at their annual meeting the stockholders gave initial approval. Formal ratification of interim agreements, of the proposed board of directors, of certain joint expenditures, and of other details, were finalized in March and quickly followed by approval of the Comptroller of the Currency in Washington. Then came the intensive physical activity of moving and the opening for business on April 1, 1956, of First City National Bank of Houston.

At the end of First City National's opening day the total deposits came to slightly less than $600 million. Steady and continuous growth in every aspect of its operation began at that point. The leadership of its Senior Chairman, Judge James A. Elkins, was from the beginning heartily supported by Vice-Senior Chairman P.P. Butler, by Chairman W.A. Kirkland, and by President James A. Elkins, Jr., all acting under the strong boards of directors and advisors chosen from the directorates of the merging institutions. Success rewarded the efforts of these men and of many other able officers and employees working together for the first time.

Looking back on the picture of two Houston banks in 1934 one sees the First National working steadily out of the trials of its reorganization, the City National, respected for its Depression performance, setting out with vigor for two decades of amazing growth. They come together in the consolidation of 1956, each making its special contribution to the First City National Bank, Houston's largest financial institution, leader now in a holding company known as First City Bancorporation of Texas, Inc., owner of many banks across Texas, with substantial international activities and with totals as of December 31, 1974, of $3,407,001,000 in deposits and $4,067,035,000 in assets. With the economic outlook and growth potential of both Houston and Texas, what does not the future hold for First City National Bank and First City Bancorporation?

Appendix

*Original Stockholders, First National Bank
of Houston*

February 16, 1866

J.T. Brady William Brady	J.T. & Wm. Brady	Commission Merchants
S.L. Allen H.R. Percy William Fulton	S.L. Allen & Co.	Receiving & Forwarding Agents Commission Merchants
P.J. Willis R.S. Willis	P.J. Willis & Bro.	Merchants
T.M. Bagby	Cotton Factor & Commission Merchant	
Wm. Clark	Dry Goods	
A.H. Torbert	Agent, H. & T.C. R.R. Co.	
H.R. Allen	Allen & Heitmann, Merchants	
P. Reynaud	Merchant	
Wm. N. Cooke	Bank Cashier	
T.W. House	Dry Goods, Groceries	
D. Wenar	Dry Goods, Clothing, Shoes	
L.J. Latham	Merchant	
H.H. Milby		
G.A. Forsgard	Boots and Shoes	
Paul Bremond	H. & T.C. R.R. Co.	
J.R. Morris	Merchant	
C.J. Grainger	Lumber	
A. Whitaker	Merchant	
P.W. Gray	Lawyer	
I.S. Roberts	Chief Justice, Harris County	

J.C. Drescher E. Schmidt	E. Schmidt & Co.	Hardware & Cutlery
A. Somerville Muter Miller	Miller & Somerville	Commission Merchants
N.W. Bush J.C. Cabeen	Bush & Cabeen	Merchants
M. Reichman S. Meyer	M. Reichman & Co.	Auctioneers and Merchants
T.W. Whitmarsh W. L. Macatee	Macatee & Whitmarsh	Cotton Factors & Commission Merchants
Louis Pless H.H. Haynie	Louis Pless & Co.	Cotton & Wool Factors
E.H. Cushing		
E.H. Cushing E.W. Cave	E.H. Cushing & Co.	Books, Stationery, Printing
B.F. Peel E.H. Dumble	Peel & Dumble	Cotton & Wool Factors
E.B.H. Schneider H.B. Berleth W.A. Pettit	Schneider, Pettit & Berleth	Storage & Commission Merchants
S.L. Hohenthal	Auctioneer & Merchant	

Directors, First National Bank
of Houston

1866 - 1933

T.M. Bagby	February, 1866 - January, 1868
J.T. Brady	February, 1866 - January, 1867
William Clark	February, 1866 - January, 1867
William Fulton	February, 1866 - January, 1867
S.L. Hohenthal	February, 1866 - January, 1868
H.R. Percy	February, 1866 - January, 1875
M. Reichman	February, 1866 - January, 1867
I.S. Roberts	February, 1866 - January, 1867
R.S. Willis	February, 1866 - January, 1869
B.A. Shepherd	January, 1867 - December, 1891
R. Brewster	January, 1867 - January, 1868
	January, 1869 - April, 1869

(continued on next page)

G.A. Forsgard	January, 1867 - January, 1868
C.C. Speers	January, 1868 - January, 1869
L.J. Latham	January, 1868 - January, 1869
	April, 1869 - January, 1870
	January, 1871 - March, 1886
H.S. Fox	January, 1869 - March, 1869
A. Wettermark	January, 1869 - December, 1875
J.J. Hendley	March, 1869 - January, 1871
	January, 1875 - January, 1877
George Baker	January, 1870 - January, 1871
	January, 1874 - January, 1879
M. Jacobs	January, 1871 - January, 1874
August Bering	January, 1876 - January, 1908
Conrad Bering	January, 1877 - January, 1879
O.L. Cochran	January, 1879 - February, 1914
A.P. Root	January, 1879 - February, 1908
F.T. Shepherd	April, 1886 - January, 1890
W.H. Palmer	January, 1890 - September, 1902
Mrs. M.L. Roberts	January, 1892 - January, 1906
W.S. Cochran	September, 1902 - May, 1933
Mrs. W.H. Palmer	January, 1906 - January, 1907
J.T. Scott	January, 1907 - May, 1933
E.A. Palmer	January, 1908 - August, 1908
Mrs. A.P. Root	March, 1908 - August, 1908
W.H. Kirkland	August, 1908 - May, 1914
E.A. Peden	August, 1908 - May, 1933
H.R. Eldridge	January, 1910 - January, 1913
E.L. Neville	January, 1913 - May, 1933
Oscar Wells	January, 1913 - October, 1914
F.M. Law	January, 1915 - May, 1933
F.E. Russell	January, 1915 - April, 1923
F.A. Root	January, 1919 - January, 1927
Sam R. Lawder	January, 1923 - May, 1933
O.W. Jackson	January, 1924 - February, 1929
W.A. Kirkland	January, 1927 - May, 1933
M.D. Jenkins	February, 1929 - May, 1933

Officers, First National Bank of Houston

1866 - 1933

Chairman of the Board

J.T. Scott	1930 - 1933

President

T.M. Bagby	1866 - 1867

(continued on next page)

B.A. Shepherd	1867 - 1891
A.P. Root	1892 - 1908
O.L. Cochran	1908 - 1914
J.T. Scott	1914 - 1929
F.M. Law	1930 - 1933

Chairman, Executive Committee

| E.L. Neville | 1932 - 1933 |

Vice President

R.S. Willis	1866 - 1867
H.R. Percy	1868 - 1873
L.J. Latham	1874 - 1886
August Bering	1886 - 1889
O.L. Cochran	1890 - 1908
J.T. Scott	1908 - 1914
H.R. Eldridge	1910 - 1912
Oscar Wells	1913 - 1914
W.S. Cochran	1913 - 1933
F.M. Law	1915 - 1929
F.E. Russell	1923 - 1923
S.R. Lawder	1923 - 1933
W.A. Kirkland	1930 - 1933

Cashier

William Fulton	1866 (Pro Tem)
William Cooke	1866 - 1867
A. Wettermark	1867 - 1875
A.P. Root	1876 - 1891
W.H. Palmer	1892 - 1902
J.T. Scott	1902 - 1908
W.S. Cochran	1908 - 1913
F.E. Russell	1913 - 1922
O.W. Jackson	1923 - 1929
M.D. Jenkins	1929 - 1933

Assistant Vice President

H.L. Darton	1925 - 1933
J.W. Hazard	1927 - 1933
W.A. Kirkland	1928 - 1929
H.B. Bringhurst	1928 - 1933
M.D. Jenkins	1928 - 1929
C.C. Hall	1930 - 1933
D.B. Lacy	1930 - 1933
G.G. Timmins	1930 - 1933

Comptroller

| H.A. Carey | 1930 - 1933 |

Auditor

H.A. Carey	1927 - 1929

Assistant Cashiers

F. Mohl	1869 (3 mos.)
F.T. Shepherd	1884 - 1889
W.H. Palmer	1890 - 1891
W.E. Hertford	1896 - 1898
	1908 - 1912
J.T. Scott	1894 (1 mo.)
	1898 - 1902
W.S. Cochran	1904 - 1908
F.A. Root	1906 - 1907
E.A. Palmer	1908
F.E. Russell	1909 - 1912
G.G. Timmins	1912 - 1929
J.L. Russell	1912 - 1923
J.W. Hazard	1913 - 1926
H.B. Bringhurst	1913 - 1927
O.W. Jackson	1919 - 1922
W.A. Kirkland	1922 - 1927
H.T. McClung	1923 - 1933
Carl C. Hall	1924 - 1929
D.B. Lacy	1924 - 1929
M.D. Jenkins	1924 - 1927
T.L. Powell	1924 - 1926
H.R. Eldridge, Jr.	1926 - 1933
C. Meadows	1930 - 1933
D.U. Cunningham	1930 - 1933
J.A. Haralson	1930 - 1933

Original Stockholders, First National Bank in Houston

May 3, 1933

E.S. Boyles
H.B. Bringhurst
J.S. Cochran
W.S. Cochran
D.U. Cunningham
C.C. Hall
J.A. Haralson

(continued on next page)

J.W. Hazard
W.A. Kirkland
D.B. Lacy
F.M. Law
D.P. Neville
E.L. Neville
C.V. Peden
E.A. Peden
F.S. Roberts
J.T. Scott

Directors, First National Bank in Houston

1933 — 1956

J.T. Scott	1933 - 1955
E.A. Peden	1933 - 1934
E.L. Neville	1933 - 1937
F.M. Law	1933 - 1956
S.R. Lawder	1933 - 1943
W.S. Cochran	1933 - 1951
W.A. Kirkland	1933 - 1956
M.D. Jenkins	1933 - 1956
D.T. Ray	1935 - 1943
T.W. Gregory, Jr.	1943 - 1956
J.H. Crooker	1944 - 1956
J.W. Evans	1944 - 1956
J.H. Kurth, Jr.	1944 - 1956
George Sawtelle	1944 - 1956
W.A. Sherman	1944 - 1950
P.P. Butler	1944 - 1956
G.R. Brown	1945 - 1956
T.H. Monroe	1945 - 1956
Ernest Cockrell	1946 - 1947
C.M. Dow	1946 - 1950
J.H. Freeman	1946 - 1956
J.M. Jackson	1946 - 1952
D.E. Japhet	1946 - 1956
A.H. King	1946 - 1947
H.M. Wilkins	1946 - 1953
J.A. Wilkins	1946 - 1956
Wallace Wilson	1946 - 1956
Isaac Arnold	1947 - 1956
L.H. Smith	1948 - 1956
J.H. Russell	1950 - 1956
R.W. Henderson	1951 - 1956
Louis Letzerich	1952 - 1956
H.L. Autrey	1953 - 1956

(continued on next page)

W.T. Doherty	1953 - 1956
Henry Oliver	1953 - 1956

Officers, First National Bank in Houston

1933 - 1956

Chairman of the Advisory Committee

J.T. Scott	1945 - 1955

Consultation Chairman

F.M. Law	1955 - 1956

Chairman of the Board

J.T. Scott	1933 - 1944
F.M. Law	1945 - 1954
P.P. Butler	1955 - 1956

Vice-Chairman of the Board

J.Λ. Wilkins	1946 - 1954
J.Λ. Freeman	1952 - 1956

President

F.M. Law	1933 - 1944
P.P. Butler	1945 - 1954
W.A. Kirkland	1955 - 1956

Chairman of the Executive Committee

E.L. Neville	1933 - 1937
W.A. Kirkland	1945 - 1954

Executive Vice-President

W.A. Kirkland	1946 - 1954
H.M. Wilkins	1946 - 1951
M.D. Jenkins	1955 - 1956

Senior Vice-President

W.S. Cochran	1946 - 1948
M.D. Jenkins	1944 - 1954

(continued on next page)

T.W. Gregory, Jr.	1951 - 1956
Henry Oliver	1954 - 1956
A.E. Cleere	1956
(and Comptroller)	

First Vice-President

S.R. Lawder	1933 - 1943

Vice-President

W.S. Cochran	1933 - 1945
M.D. Jenkins	1933 - 1944
(and Cashier)	
W.A. Kirkland	1933 - 1944
T.W. Gregory, Jr.	1943 - 1950
H.R. Eldridge, Jr.	1945 - 1956
(and Cashier)	1945 - 1954
A.J. Martin	1945 - 1947
A.H. King	1946 - 1947
Henry Oliver	1946 - 1953
J.A. Haralson	1947 - 1956
Louis Letzerich	1948 - 1956
E.M. Reed	1948 - 1956
A.E. Cleere	1949 - 1955
(and Comptroller)	
T.H. Mattingly	1949 - 1952
J.L. Andrew	1949 - 1956
Theo Ahrenbeck	1950 - 1956
(and Cashier)	1955 - 1956
W.D. Black, Jr.	1950 - 1956
Charles Celaya	1950 - 1956
J.D. Lea	1951 - 1956
W.A. Daniel	1951 - 1956
R.C. Cardner	1951 - 1956
W.N. Sick	1952 - 1956
A.E. Joekel	1952 - 1956
P.T. Good	1952 - 1956
H.B. Clay	1952 - 1956
Grover Ellis, Jr.	1954 - 1956
C.C. Thrift	1955 - 1956
J.M. Golibart	1956
G.C. Barnett	1956
R.L. Lewis, Jr.	1956

Assistant Vice-President

H.L. Darton	1933 - 1940
J.W. Hazard	1933
H.B. Bringhurst	1933 - 1948
G.G. Timmins	1933
D.B. Lacy	1933
C.C. Hall	1933 - 1954

(continued on next page)

R.L. Tilly	1939 - 1945
H.R. Eldridge, Jr.	1941 - 1944
H.A. Carey	1941 - 1944
J.A. Haralson	1945 - 1946
Clarence Meadows	1945 - 1951
D.U. Cunningham	1945 - 1955
T.H. Mattingly	1945 - 1951
W.N. Sick	1946
Theo Ahrenbeck	1946 - 1949
Louis Letzerich	1946 - 1947
Ray Winstead	1946
Paul Barkley	1946 - 1947
J.L. Andrew	1947 - 1948
C.C. Thrift	1948 - 1954
P.T. Good	1948 - 1951
Allen Repsdorph	1948 - 1956
L.E. Fogarty	1948 - 1949
W.D. Black, Jr.	1948 - 1949
J.D. Lea	1949 - 1950
J.K. Deason	1950 - 1956
A.E. Joekel	1950 - 1951
M.B. Patterson	1950 - 1956
J.L. Everett	1950 - 1956
R.C. Cardner	1950
W.E. Bridgforth	1951 - 1956
Mrs. Jackie Greer	1952 - 1956
J.M. Golibart	1952 - 1955
C.F. Tuttle	1952 - 1956
J.W. Wiese	1953 - 1954
Grover Ellis, Jr.	1953
R.L. Lewis, Jr.	1953 - 1955
G.C. Barnett	1954 - 1955
Bill Henry	1955 - 1956

Assistant Cashier

H.T. McClung	1933 - 1941
H.R. Eldridge, Jr.	1933 - 1940
J.A. Haralson	1933 - 1944
Clarence Meadows	1933 - 1944
D.U. Cunningham	1933 - 1944
R.L. Tilly	1938 - 1939
F.C. Guthrie	1939 - 1941
W.N. Sick	1941 - 1945
Louis Letzerich	1941 - 1945
T.H. Mattingly	1942 - 1944
A.E. Joekel	1945 - 1949
M.B. Patterson	1945 - 1949
C.C. Thrift	1945 - 1947
Theo Ahrenbeck	1945
Allen Repsdorph	1945 - 1947
P.T. Good	1945 - 1947
L.E. Fogarty	1945 - 1947
W.E. Sprague	1945 - 1956
W.E. Bridgforth	1946 - 1954

(continued on next page)

J.L. Everett	1946 - 1949
F.H. Matthews	1946 - 1956
W.A. Miller	1946 - 1956
J.H. Wiese	1946 - 1952
J.K. Deason	1948 - 1949
Mrs. Jackie Greer	1949 - 1951
Herve Burghard	1950 - 1956
J.M. Golibart	1950 - 1951
J.H. Brown	1950 - 1956
C.F. Tuttle	1951
H.M. Jackson	1953 - 1956
W.C.W. Hobbs	1955 - 1956

Comptroller

H.A. Carey	1933 - 1940
A. E. Cleere	1945 - 1948

Auditor

A.E. Cleere	1941 - 1944
B.O. Bruner	1955 - 1956

Assistant Auditor

R.J. Runnels	1955 - 1956

Sr. Vice-President & Trust Officer

C.D. Simmons	1952 - 1956

Vice-President and Trust Officer

D.T. Ray	1934 - 1943
J.M. Jackson	1946 - 1952
L.H. Thomas	1948 - 1956

Trust Officer

D.T. Ray	1933 - 1934
L.H. Thomas	1940 - 1947
J.C. Faris	1948 - 1956
D.D. Peden	1948 - 1956
G.F. Neff	1956

Assistant Trust Officer

F.C. Guthrie	1936 - 1938
J.C. Faris	1945 - 1947
Mrs. Sarita Flynn	1951 - 1956
R.W. Malone	1953 - 1956
G.F. Neff	1953 - 1955

Index